THE WICKED TRUTH

WHEN GOOD PEOPLE DO BAD THINGS

Suzanne Ross

The Wicked Truth Web site: http://www.thewickedtruth.com
The Raven Foundation Web site: http://www.ravenfoundation.org

Book Design by Brandon Jameson, A+B Works.

ISBN 978-1-60402-982-6

To my parents, Marie and Jack DeCarlo,
who embody the great virtues of compassion
and humility. You are my inspiration.

For I do not do the good I want, but the evil I do not want is what I do.

ROMANS 7:19

Returning violence for violence multiples violence, adding deeper darkness to a night already devoid of stars. Darkness cannot drive out darkness; only light can do that. Hate cannot drive out hate; only love can do that.

MARTIN LUTHER KING JR.

WARNING TO ALL READERS:
THERE ARE SPOILERS AFOOT.

PROCEED WITH CAUTION.

TABLE OF CONTENTS

INTRODUCTION

In the sweltering summer of 1988 my husband, Keith, and I moved our family from New Jersey to a Chicago suburb. It was a business move – Keith was an options trader and Chicago was the place to be for the options business. What we didn't know was that we were in for the experience of a lifetime. Two years later the Chicago Bulls, led by Michael Jordan, would begin an eight year run in which they won six National Basketball Association Championships. When we moved I couldn't tell a backboard from a floorboard, but that was to change in a hurry.

My family and I got caught up in the Bulls mania. City and suburbs were obsessed with the team, agonizing over every loss, dissecting every substitution, and cursing every referee who dared to call a penalty on our beloved Michael. I tracked players' stats and critiqued coaching decisions as if I were a basketball professional. Then an odd dynamic developed in our marriage. Whenever the kids were driving us crazy or the checking account was perilously low, Keith or I could head off an argument by asking, "What about them Bulls?" Tension was transformed into camaraderie as we excitedly shared our reactions to the most recent game. We began to joke that the Bulls were better than a marriage counselor.

The best time of the year was during the playoff rounds in April and May. A peace descended on the city much like the peace in our marriage. Sure, Chicago fans were anxious about our chances, but you could repeat that reliable phrase, "What about them Bulls?" to a complete stranger and feel like you'd just bumped into an old friend. Waiters, checkout clerks and grocery baggers, people waiting with you in line to renew your drivers license – it didn't matter who, when or where – you shared a special bond with them because of the Chicago Bulls. All differences melted in the heat of our passion for the team. It was like Christmas in May – all the world seemed peaceful, loving, and full of promise.

I began to wonder how a winning basketball team could create peace and harmony in both a marriage and a city as diverse as Chicago. For a while the answer seemed obvious. Being fans gave us all something in common. When something divided us, the Bulls were there to unite us. Like the weather, the Bulls were a great icebreaker, and because they were winning, well, it made us all feel happy. Winning is fun, after all. But as the Bulls' amazing championship run was ending I was introduced to the work of the contemporary cultural theorist, René Girard, and I realized that there was more to it than that.

As I read his work, I became aware that the peace we were experiencing had a dark side. As we celebrated each championship season, our joy was matched by the nearly invisible grief of our defeated foe. We knew it was there but we didn't dwell on it. At the end of the final game, the TV cameras revealed the downcast faces of the losers and if we chose, we could see and feel the depression in the losing locker room. But in my house there was so much cheering and celebrating that we easily turned away from such pictures. We quieted down to hear interviews with the Bulls players and coaches, but we didn't bother to listen to what the losing coach said – unless it was to congratulate us and tell us what a great team we had. Dwelling too much on the grief of the losers would have dampened our celebration.

Looking at the experience of winning with the Bulls this way opened my eyes. I realized that the peace Chicagoans were experiencing and the way we had achieved it revealed something about how all peaceful communities have always achieved and kept the peace. The Bulls' championship had functioned like one of those "reenactment" television commercials that use actors to play real people. As real as the suffering experienced by the losing team was, I came to see that it was a pale imitation of the real suffering playing out beyond the confines of the stadium. Perhaps there was value in lingering in the loser's locker room. Rather than ruin my good time, it might be the first step toward a more inclusive community of peace.

After studying and living with Girard's theories for many years, I came across the musical, *Wicked*. In the opening moments of the show, the Ozians are celebrating the defeat of their enemy, the Wicked Witch. Their triumphant song reminded me of Chicago's championship celebrations. But unlike the Bulls' victory celebrations, this one is interrupted. Rather than hearing from the victorious team of Dorothy and her friends in a kind of post-game, winning locker room wrap up, the Ozians are told the loser's story. The camera zooms in on the loser's locker room and doesn't turn away for two hours. As I watched the relationship between Glinda and Elphaba change from a stormy whirlwind of bruised egos, gossip and petty resentments into one of true love and friendship, I saw a metaphor for how my own life was being transformed by Girard's ideas.

This book is my attempt to share with you the insights I have learned about building peaceful relationships. I am indebted not only to the incredible genius of René Girard, but also to the scholars and teachers of his theories who have been so kind and generous toward me over the years. I am forever grateful to Gil Bailie, Sandor Goodhart, Andrew McKenna, Ann Astell, Tom Ryba, Paul Nuechterlein and James Alison for the quality of their scholarship and the pleasure of their friendship and support. More than anything, they have taught me by example what it means to live in a spirit of kindness and compassion, judging little and loving much. Much is owed to my late friend and mentor, Rev. C. David Owens, who introduced me to Girard and whose life was a vivid example of the risks and dangers of daring to speak the truth. I am indebted to Kyrra Rankine for her thoughtful editing and to Erik Orton for his commitment to this project. And without my husband Keith's sense of humor, unshakable faith in me, his passion for the Bulls, for Girard and for *Wicked*, this would have been a lonely and impossible undertaking.

I would also like to express my deep gratitude and admiration for the visionary creative team that brought *Wicked* to the stage: Marc Platt, Universal Pictures, The Araca Group, Jon B. Platt and David Stone, producers; music and lyrics by Stephen Schwartz; book by Winnie Holzman; directed by Joe Mantello; music arrangements by

Alex Lacamoire and Stephen Oremus; music coordinator, Michael Keller; orchestrations by William David Brohn; music director, Stephen Oremus; musical staging by Wayne Cilento. By making a loser's tale of defeat and suffering as entertaining and uplifting as a victory parade, they have helped illuminate a long hidden obstacle to genuine peace.

I

Looking at the World Through Green Colored Glasses

He opened the big box, and Dorothy saw that it was filled with spectacles of every size and shape. All of them had green glasses in them. The Guardian of the gates found a pair that would just fit Dorothy and put them over her eyes... When they were on, Dorothy could not take them off had she wished, but of course she did not want to be blinded by the glare of the Emerald City, so she said nothing.

L. FRANK BAUM,
The Wonderful Wizard of Oz

I just mean, Glinda, is it possible we could be living our entire adult lives under someone's spell?

MAGUIRE, *Wicked*

Repetition does not transform a lie into a truth.

FRANKLIN D. ROOSEVELT,
Radio address, October 26, 1939

The blockbuster Broadway musical *Wicked*[1] opens with the celebration of a death. As the curtain rises, the stage fills with actors singing in unison about the defeat of an enemy of all the people. Their wild, exuberant chorus echoes throughout the theater:

Good News! She's Dead!
The Witch of the West is dead!
The Wickedest Witch there ever was,
The enemy of all of us here in Oz,
Is dead!
Good News!
Good News![2]

Of course, the audience recognizes her by name – the Wicked Witch of the West – a woman so wicked that the adjective is part of her name. We know her as the enemy of the good people of Oz, the wondrously colorful land of the classic movie[3] to which Dorothy of black and white Kansas is transported via twister and a bump on the head. Those of us of a certain age remember our excitement when, in the deep silence after the tornado, Dorothy slowly opened the door of her damaged house to glimpse the world beyond the rainbow. The profusion of color dazzled us, and we were unsurprised to learn that while this world contained extreme goodness, the evil here was more intense as well.

Among my favorite moments from the movie is the gruesome melting of the Wicked Witch. As she dies slowly, the Witch rubs her bony hands together and cries, "Who ever thought a little girl like you could destroy my beautiful wickedness?"[4] Dorothy seemed so meek and powerless up to that point, and the Witch so ruthlessly evil. I can still recall the fear I felt as the Witch pursued Dorothy and her friends through the corridors, the monkeys screeching wildly behind her. I agreed with the Witch: How could a little girl defeat such wickedness? I was terrified. But the forces of good, however puny, emerged from the battle victorious. I was catapulted from deathly fear to joyous celebration as fast as it takes a little girl to throw a pail of water, and I couldn't have been happier. When Dorothy returns home safely to

A CLASSIC TALE OF GOOD AND EVIL

The classic movie, *The Wizard of Oz,* tells the familiar story of good conquering evil by using a little girl to defeat a wicked witch. Just to refresh your memory, here's a quick summary of the 1939 movie starring Judy Garland as Dorothy:

Dorothy is an innocent young girl in search of her heart's desire. She gets bumped on the head during a tornado and when she wakes up, finds herself in a strange land far from home. Her arrival causes the accidental death of a wicked witch, whose powerful magic shoes she comes to possess. As Dorothy tries to return to her home, she makes three unlikely friends, who are also in search of their hearts' desires. The foursome encounters many adventures on their journey to ask the ruler of the kingdom, a wonderfully good wizard, for help.

The Wizard lives in a grand palace in the capital city and he agrees to help Dorothy and her friends on one condition – that they bring him the broom of the Wicked Witch of the West. The four friends know that they will have to kill the Witch to get her broom, and although they feel frightened and unequal to the task, they also feel they have no choice. The Witch has been pursuing them on their journey to the Emerald City because she wants the magic shoes that once belonged to her now dead sister.

The friends have a benefactor, however, in the Good Witch of the North, who assists them as they travel to the city's capital. With more than a bit of good fortune, they manage to kill the Wicked Witch and return to the Wizard with the broom. Unfortunately, the Wizard turns out to be a humbug with no power to grant their wishes. Amazingly, they find out that they already possessed the very things they went to the Wizard to receive. Dorothy is transported home with a click of her magic heels to discover that it was all just a bad dream. And so, the story ends quite happily.

discover that the evil she encountered was only a dream, it made my world feel a bit safer, too. It is a movie ending I have savored all my life.

Then in 2003, I saw an ad for a new Broadway musical declaring, "So much happened before Dorothy dropped in!" Well, okay, I thought. Maybe things did happen in Oz before Dorothy got there, but what more do I need to know? I had been reassured by the movie's happy ending asserting that witches and goblins lived somewhere over the rainbow, not under my bed or in my closet. I was satisfied that good little girls could conquer evil. Whatever happened in Oz in this supposed imaginary "before" time was of no interest to the little girl who still lived inside me.

My adult self was equally doubtful – I could not imagine any way to improve on the story or the music of the well-known classic. The writing team for the musical – composer Stephen Schwartz and author Winnie Holzman – were impressive, but I wondered how they could compete with the songs "Somewhere Over the Rainbow" and "Ding Dong the Witch is Dead," or lines like, "I'll get you my pretty – and your little dog too!" I had not yet read the novel by Gregory Maguire[5] that inspired the stage production for much the same reasons. I felt sure the movie had satisfied my need to spend time with Dorothy, the Wizard, the Witches (good and bad), the Scarecrow, Tin Man and Cowardly Lion. Even the Wicked Witch of the West I knew as intimately as a dear friend. How could Gregory Maguire or the writers and producers of *Wicked* improve something that was already perfect?

If I had read the children's book that inspired the movie, I might have understood what was motivating these writers. L. Frank Baum's novel, *The Wonderful Wizard of Oz*,[6] first published in 1900, is not at all like the movie. They both contain the same characters and settings, and each deals with the theme of good conquering evil, but the conclusion each reaches about this conquest is quite different. Baum's novel hesitates to reach any solid conclusions at all, raising more questions than it answers. It hints repeatedly that something deeper is going on beneath the surface of this epic battle, a hidden truth that is being concealed. His book is laced with clues that something is not quite right in the Land of Oz, and there exist deceptions and lies that we would do well to uncover. Reading Baum's novel is an invitation to go sleuthing, an invitation both Maguire and the creators of *Wicked* eagerly accepted.

I'm glad they did. My beloved movie does not do justice to the revelatory potential of Baum's novel. His story is more than a child's fairy tale. It provides us with a rich, complex metaphor for the world we inhabit this side of the rainbow. As I began to read, I questioned the rhyme and reason of what occurred in Oz, but by the end of the novel I wondered if hidden in the text was an even more compelling question: What can we know about good and evil in our own world?

The creators of the movie transformed Baum's admirable creative effort into a sweet tale that ends with a satisfying moral sound bite: There's no place like home. There is no such sweet summation in Baum's version. In Baum's original, Dorothy does not get bumped on the head and does not fall unconscious on the bed as the house is lifted up into the cyclone. She stays wide awake as the house flies up into the air, with no suggestion at all that she is dreaming the entire episode. As if to dispel any such interpretation, Baum makes clear at the end of the story that when Dorothy returns home she finds not the old house that had flown to Oz, but a "new farm-house Uncle Henry built after the cyclone had carried away the old one."[7] This ending made it difficult for me to explain away all that happened by interpreting it as a dream or a child's fantasy. Was I to believe that this story really happened just the way Baum was telling it? This fairy tale was like no other in the way it thwarted my attempts at easy interpretations.

To complicate things, just as I thought I knew a character, the ground shifted and my assumptions changed. If I paid attention to what the characters said, I learned one thing. But that understanding was quickly challenged when I observed those characters' actions. In this way the story seems to insist that we not accept things at face value. Perhaps Baum is inviting us to question if the truth we all know and accept might in fact be an elaborate lie.

Have you ever had the uneasy feeling that you were being lied to? Usually liars are quite good at concealing their lie beneath a layer or two of truth so that we are thrown off balance, accepting everything they say because part of it makes sense. A truly good liar believes in his lie with all his heart, deceiving not just others, but himself as well. There are classic lies that we have all heard, like the parent who beats

CONSPIRACY THEORIES

Americans love conspiracy theories. This tongue in cheek survey appeared in a Sylvia cartoon:

What is your favorite paranoid theory?

1. "Elements of our government assisted in the September 11 attacks because they wanted war in Iraq."

2. "During Katrina, certain levees were blown up to protect wealthy areas."

3. "The government is withholding proof of intelligent life on other planets."

4. "I'm pretty sure they're all true."*

Reading these theories, I'm reminded of the expression, "Just because I'm paranoid doesn't mean they aren't out to get me!" Jokes aside, we can't help but wonder if there might be a kernel of truth hidden in all these unbelievable tales. After all, they seem to be claiming that our ignorance is contributing to the success of evil forces. What if our refusal to believe is the biggest threat of all to our peace and security?

I have often wondered if conspiracy theorists are giving expression to a collective bad feeling that we are living a lie on a grand scale. If we can manage to not take their surface claims seriously, we may discover in them a universal theme: blindness on the part of good people to an evil in their midst. Like Baum's novel, they invite us to search for the hidden truth behind the things we accept at face value.

* Nicole Hollander, *Sylvia*, cartoon. *Chicago Tribune*, 26 Sept. 2006: 6.

his child and says, "It's for your own good." This parent believes his lie so thoroughly that the child believes it, too, and we get the dynamic of an abused child who refuses to seek help in order to protect his parent. Or the alcoholic who denies the addiction that is obvious to all who know him, or the racist who believes the world must be saved from infection by an inferior race. Each of these lies, if told relentlessly and with enough conviction, can create a world in which the lie becomes the truth and anyone who dares to tell the truth is accused of being a liar. With the truth concealed, lies can turn a society upside down, and inside out, like Baum's fairy tale landscape where everyone says one thing (claiming to be good) and does another (behaving badly).

As I read further, I began to realize why this children's novel is considered a classic and why it was worth analyzing the meanings beneath the surface. It may seem odd to include a child's fairy tale in a category that contains Shakespeare's plays and Dostoevsky's novels. But a story becomes a classic because it contains an excess of meaning. That is, a reader can return to it again and again and find a new application allowing them to read the old words in a new way. A classic has longevity because it raises the questions that are important to human life no matter the time period or physical place.

19th century Russian novels and 16th century English plays have meaning for me – an American in the 21st century – because those stories deal with questions that matter to me today – the meaning and purpose of life, the nature of love, how to live with integrity, war and peace. Stories that deal honestly and unflinchingly with these subjects are the classic stories that speak across the generations. Baum's novel raises such a question, one as worthy of our attention today as 100 years ago: Are there some lies about good and evil that we should begin to question?

As I read the novel critically, I discovered signposts that pointed toward the heart of the story, the place where the hidden meaning might be found. The Emerald City is located at the center of this imaginary landscape as the goal for Dorothy and her friends on their quest.[8]
I interpreted this as a signal like the X on a treasure map, marking the spot directly over Oz's green capital. If I could gain access to the central

truths hidden by the Wizard's lies and devoutly believed in by its citizens, perhaps I could find the truth Baum wanted his readers to uncover.

How does Baum describe the City of Emeralds? He presents it to us as a culturally rich seat of power wielded on behalf of goodness. It is also the place where desires are fulfilled – at least that is the promise made to Dorothy and her friends. It is a city that is confident in its ability to distinguish good from evil, friends from enemies, the wicked from the wonderful. From all outward appearances, it is a city at peace with itself and with the world outside its walls. What we think we know about the peace and goodness of the Emerald City – and the peace and goodness of our own communities – is the lie the novel unmasks.

Without attempting to summarize the entire plot of Baum's novel, I will highlight some of the places where I felt as if I were witnessing an impressive sleight of hand. Here are some examples of the way the novel reveals, with a wink and a nod, that the characters are constantly telling us lies about themselves and their world. As we explore them together, we will be prompted to ask questions that no one in the novel is asking.

THE "WONDERFUL" WIZARD?

Early in the book, when Dorothy lands in Munchkinland, she meets an old lady who says she is the Witch of the North. She tells Dorothy about the Wizard, assuring the girl that the Wizard is good and will help her return home. But when Dorothy finally arrives at the entrance to the Emerald City, the Guardian of the gate tells her that Oz is "powerful and terrible," not good. The Wizard himself, when she finally meets him, behaves badly. The only reason he agrees to see Dorothy at all is that the Guardian tells him the girl is wearing the silver (not ruby, as in the movie) shoes of the now deceased Witch of the East, and that she has a mark on her forehead, the sign of a kiss given by the Witch of the North. The Wizard recognizes these as signs of power and begins maneuvering to use the arrival of this girl to his advantage.

When Dorothy asks for his help to return to Kansas, he says, "You have no right to expect me to send you back to Kansas unless you do something for me in return. In this country everyone must pay for everything he gets."[9] The thing she must do, of course, is kill the Wicked Witch of the West. Why does the Wizard want the Witch killed? He tells Dorothy it is because she is wicked – tremendously wicked – and deserves to die. However, the reader discovers ten pages later that there has been a war between the Wizard and the Witch of the West and the Witch has won, driving the Wizard "out of the land of the West." This news reveals that the Wizard is neither good nor wonderful, nor generous or kind. He is, in fact, a power-grabbing ruler who thinks only of his own political and military needs. Though his self-serving title tells us he is Wonderful, the novel warns us that the title is nothing more than a publicity stunt. The Ruler of Oz wants us to believe that he is good, so he remains hidden behind his smoky mask, inaccessible to all but a few.

THE "EMERALD" CITY?

As Dorothy and her friends approach the Emerald City, they must overcome many obstacles. The city itself is protected by a dark forest filled with dangers: a field of poisonous poppies, a broad and wild river, and a great, green wall with a locked gate. Though the city appears green from the outside, in order to enter the friends agreed to have green-tinted glasses fastened onto their heads. They are locked in place with a key that is held by the Guardian of the gate. As long as they are inside the city, they are forced, as are all the residents of the city, to wear them. Why? They are told by the Guard that if they "did not wear the spectacles the brightness and glory of the Emerald City would blind" them.[10] Of course, while inside the city wearing the glasses, everything appears green. Once outside, with the glasses removed, Dorothy notices that she "still wore the pretty silk dress she had put on in the palace, but now, to her surprise, she found it was no longer green, but pure white. The ribbon around Toto's neck had also lost its green color and became as white as Dorothy's dress."[11] Baum tells us nothing more, but we are left to wonder: Is the Emerald City a place of wonder and marvelous joy, or is the beauty and promise of the city simply an illusion?

IF I ONLY HAD A BRAIN

Dorothy's three friends – the Scarecrow, the Tin Man, and the Lion – appear in the novel much the same as they do in the movie. They are characters in search of missing character traits, willing to brave danger and commit murder in order to possess the things they profess to lack. Yet, throughout the novel as in the movie, they seem to already be in possession of the things they so desperately want. Baum gives many examples of the Scarecrow's wise actions, the Tin Man's compassionate feelings, and the Lion's courageous nature, yet not one of them believes he holds these qualities until after the Wicked Witch is dead. Why? Why was it necessary for them to kill someone in order to recognize who they truly were all along? If they had believed in themselves from the beginning, might they have been able to ask the question no one dared ask the Wizard, the question that Schwartz and Holzman ask in their musical: What exactly is so wicked about the Witch?

HOW WICKED IS SHE?

Baum presents us with a very wicked witch indeed. The Witch of the West is the enemy of the Wizard, having defeated him in battle and driven him out of her land where she can now rule without any constraint on her wickedness. She has her flying monkeys attack the Tin Woodman and the Scarecrow, severely injuring both of them. The Witch imprisons and starves the Lion, hoping to break his spirit and use him as a workhorse. She only keeps Dorothy alive so she can figure out how to get the silver shoes and possess their power. Yet for all her fearfulness Dorothy has always possessed all the power she needs to overcome her.

In both the movie and book, Dorothy destroys the Witch with a bucket of water. In the novel, however, it is thrown in a fit of anger after the Witch trips her and one of the silver shoes comes off. Each of them now wears one shoe, mirror images of each other, and as they face each other down, Dorothy demands that the witch return her shoe. Here is how Baum tells it:

> "I will not," retorted the Witch, "for it is now my shoe, and not yours."
>
> "You are a wicked creature!" cried Dorothy. "You have no right to take my shoe from me."
>
> "I shall keep it, just the same," said the Witch, laughing at her, "and some day I shall get the other one from you, too."
>
> This made Dorothy so very angry that she picked up the bucket of water that stood near and dashed it over the Witch, wetting her from head to foot.[12]

I wondered if Baum hoped his readers would ask a few questions about this peculiar event. Are we to accept that this is how Dorothy kills the Witch, this most terrible paragon of wickedness, that she has a child's temper tantrum and destroys her with that most fearsome of destructive weapons – moisture? How could someone so powerful be destroyed so easily? Something is not right here. Either Dorothy is not the picture of meekness she professes to be, or the Witch is not nearly the threat Dorothy has been led to believe. Which is it?

There is more to these characters and the story of their accidental meeting than I had ever imagined, and it is precisely those subtleties that comprise the more important story. Through powerful music and storytelling, *Wicked* reveals what happened in Oz before Dorothy arrived. This new version of the Oz story dares to challenge what we hold true about good and evil by boldly giving voice to the enemy of Oz, the wickedest Witch of all. It insists we listen to the story of the one whose death was viewed as necessary and just, as the only way for Dorothy and her friends to achieve their hearts' desires. It transforms the Wicked Witch of the West, from a murderer seeking to destroy Dorothy to obtain the power of the ruby slippers, into a misunderstood, unloved girl with a birth defect. How could I never have questioned the necessity of killing the Witch to make dreams come true? Why did I never wonder how the Witch came to live by herself in a dark castle with only flying monkeys for companions? What made me assume that if I were to play a role in the movie, I would be Dorothy – completely innocent and completely good?

The Witch's story does not excuse wicked deeds with sad stories of traumatized childhoods and lack of opportunity. Rather than explain evil away, it confronts the reader with our own failures to uncover evil's true hiding places. The frightening truth may be that, to paraphrase an old song, we have been looking for evil in all the wrong places and so evil is getting away scot-free.

This book will explore what the musical has to say about good and evil, and it will call into question the things we all take as unquestionable truths. At times you may feel uncomfortable or troubled, but if you are curious or courageous enough, this book will challenge the stories we love to tell about wicked witches and innocent heroines. As Glinda sings in the opening minutes of the musical, "Isn't it nice to know that good will conquer evil?" It is nice and deeply comforting, but is it good?

2

Pulling Back the Curtain

Good people make good decisions. That's why they're good people.

WAYNE LA PIERRE,
Executive Vice President of the N.R.A.

Remember that the Witch is Wicked – tremendously Wicked – and ought to be killed.

L. FRANK BAUM,
The Wonderful Wizard of Oz

...I use "myth" to refer to a special combination of fact and fantasy, one that tells of an actual violent event, but that tells of it from the perspective of the society which benefited from the violence and that therefore veils and vindicates the actual violence.

GIL BAILIE,
Violence Unveiled

Although good people can – and will – do bad things, they are still good people. This may seem like an excuse for bad behavior or like one step down the slippery slope of moral relativism. If good people can do bad things or make bad decisions, then what makes one individual good and another bad? More importantly, don't we judge ourselves by our actions?

If you are reading this book, it's safe to say that you are a good person, the type of person who takes being good seriously. You know that being good does not happen by accident, but is the result of hard work, self-discipline and making difficult choices. You want to *be* good not as an end in itself, but because you want to *do* good. If you thought you were doing bad things, well, you would have a hard time thinking of yourself as a good person.

The problem with that, of course, is that all human beings are imperfect creatures; we make mistakes and do the wrong thing all the time. Being a good person can't mean we always do the right thing, never make mistakes or hurt other people. If that were the case, no one could ever be called good. Doing the wrong thing doesn't make us bad individuals; it makes us human. If we are honest with ourselves, we can readily think of times when we did shameful things. The truth is, when you think about it, being good is not so easy or easily defined.

Except in stories. Easily and quickly telling the good guys from the bad guys is the cornerstone of traditional story telling. The heroes and villains are so completely obvious that the storyteller needs only to give us a few outward signs: white hat, clean-shaven face, and a comical relationship with his horse for the Hero; black hat, scruffy beard, and small, beady eyes for the Villain. In the movie version of Oz, good wears a tiara and evil is dressed exclusively in unfashionable black. With the distinctions between good and evil settled so quickly, the storyteller can jump right into the action, which is inevitably the battle between these two complete opposites.

The really fun part – and the reason we are addicted to these types of stories – is that, we, the audience, know without a doubt that we are on the side of the good guys. We are absolutely certain that we would never behave as reprehensibly as the bad guys. In fact, if we had the chance, we'd join the heroine and drop a house on or liquefy any witch we came across, and maybe not by accident, either. Childhood fairy tales are stories in which wicked folks are defeated by goodness: Cinderella outfoxes her evil stepmother and marries the prince; Red Riding Hood is rescued from the Big Bad Wolf when the wood cutter hacks him to pieces; the Three Little Pigs boil their huffing and puffing nemesis; and Hansel and Gretel roast their witch in the oven she had gleefully prepared for them. In all of these stories goodness conquers evil, bringing joy to all who haven't been outfoxed, hacked to pieces, boiled, baked, or liquefied.

There are modern versions of this story, of course. We pay good money at the movies to see the good guy beat the bad guy and, if the movie is done well, we feel relief and satisfaction as we vicariously share in the successful defeat of evil. There are countless movies of this type, but some examples come quickly to mind: James Bond, Terminator, Die Hard, and Mission Impossible movies[1] and the entire American Western genre, to name a few. Any stories in which the good guys are flawlessly good and their enemies are purely evil are updated versions of old fairy tales. And as in the fairy tales, any method is justified in order to defeat the threat – usually portrayed as the destruction of all life as we know it – that is posed by the evil enemies, whether they are robots or evil geniuses or amoral criminals or wicked witches.

But the musical, *Wicked*, has as its premise a delightfully wicked idea: what if instead of jumping right into the action, we need to take a step back and be sure we've identified the good and bad guys correctly? If so, we might have to ask some questions, maybe give the bad guy a chance to tell us his side of the story.

At first glance, this line of questioning might seem like a waste of time. After all, why do we need to hear the evil ravings of someone bent on destroying us? Most of the good guy/bad guy movies let the villain have a speech or two explaining his motivation, revealing his total disregard for goodness and human life. In the movie *The Wizard of Oz*, we see the Wicked Witch of the West high in her mountain fortress gleefully plotting ways to destroy Dorothy and her friends. All she wants is the ruby slippers – we hear it from her own mouth – and she doesn't care that she has to kill Dorothy to get them. She admits that it's not the killing that bothers her, but the method she will employ because of the delicate nature of the magic surrounding the ruby slippers. If Dorothy's death isn't brought about properly, the magic will be destroyed. Why give someone like that a platform from which to speak? Wouldn't that be allowing the Witch to use our own compassion against us?

Wicked's response to these questions is to wonder if the speeches attributed to the Wicked Witch of the West, and to all bad guys, are not completely accurate. Rather than being an objective account, as if they were transcribed from a tape recording of the event, what if it were a biased account of the good guys' recollections? In that case, bad guys' speeches in the movies would not be true representations of their thoughts and motives, merely the version of events that the winner gets to tell by virtue of being the winner and still alive to do the reporting.

Cultural theorists are studying the idea that the winner's version of the story obscures the loser's version. They use a word to describe the winner's story that has been used and misunderstood in modern times. The word is "myth." Many of us think of myths as powerful symbolic representations of the inner workings of the human psyche. Popular authors writing about the myths of ancient cultures such as the Greeks, Egyptians and Aztecs have described myths as springing from the human imagination and never connect them to anything that actually happened.[2] Ogres, monsters, witches, or dragons are no more real than the tales of creation that describe the world springing from the mouth of a god or life being destroyed by catastrophic floods. For these authors, though, myths contain certain truths about human psychology and should be studied as an ancient path to knowledge about our inner lives.

Others use the word myth to represent something – a story or figure – that is completely untrue. They use it synonymously with the word "legend" to describe something that we know may have a basis in truth but that has been stretched into a whopper of a lie. Like a fisherman's tale of his record-breaking catch or legendary stories of Robin Hood, King Arthur and Paul Bunyan, these sagas contain so many elements of the fantastic that we know they cannot be true. Consequently, we call them myths and dismiss their relevance as little more than minor entertainment value.

So which is it: Do mythological stories contain an element of truth or are they lies? The contemporary theorist, René Girard, has been using the

THE WORK OF RENÉ GIRARD

It is not uncommon for academics to spend their careers pursuing narrowly defined areas of research. They become quite expert at things no one can understand except those in their field. René Girard is an academic who shatters that mold by being both interdisciplinary and relevant to a wide range of readers.

He began his academic life in his native France as a historian in the 1940's. His area of interest: private life in the second half of the fifteenth century in Avignon, a perfect example of a narrow field of scholarly study. He had the opportunity to study in the United States at Indiana University and, after earning a PhD in history in 1950 the university offered him a position teaching not history, but French literature. Nevertheless, he accepted the position and what appeared to be an odd personnel decision became a turning point in his career.

To prepare for his new teaching assignment, Girard read French novelists with great interest. Cervantes, Stendhal, Flaubert and Proust were all luminaries who were praised for their distinctive styles and contributions to literature. But Girard saw more than their uniqueness. As he read, commonalities emerged that had been previously unobserved by prevailing literary scholars. This historian-turned-literature-professor discovered that each of these writers, along with the Russian novelist, Dostoevsky, was dealing with the same dynamic: the origin of conflict in human desire.

Girard's first book, *Desire, Deceit and the Novel*, presented his theory that we learn what to desire from one another, and those shared desires lead us into conflict. By continuing to study literature, anthropology, mythology and the Bible, he developed an understanding of how conflict is resolved through the use of scapegoats and the Sacrificial Mechanism.

Girard's discoveries transcended the disciplines of history and French literature, as well as the limits of academic departmentalization. His theories incorporate such diverse fields as psychology, anthropology, linguistics, theology, and education.

...continued on next page

...continued from previous page

The outcome of Girard's in-depth study is extraordinarily meaningful for the average person trying to understand themselves, their relationships, and their desires. For me, reading and studying Girard's ideas provided a pathway to begin answering my own long-held questions, such as:

How can I be good?
Does evil exist?
Is peace possible?
Do humans have an instinct for violence?
Does the end justify the means?
What is happiness and how do I pursue it?

I have had the happy fortune of meeting René Girard at the annual conference devoted to his work. I even had my picture taken with him, which I proudly display on my desk. He defies our idea of the typical academic in another way, too: He is unpretentious and genuinely interested in others, even non-academics like me. Girard insists that it is not his theory, rather that it belongs to the many great writers and thinkers who came before him who have been trying for centuries to get our attention and communicate their observations. With both clarity and humility, René Girard perceived the import and implications of their insights.

word in a way that actually combines the two meanings. For Girard, myths are the stories that get told by winners to deliberately conceal the losers' story. In that sense it is a lie, and a whopper because, not only does it omit a big part of the story, it then distorts the events to make the victor appear completely virtuous and the loser wholly wicked. But the myth contains a bit of truth, which is the key to why it gets told in the first place: The winner actually does experience a sense of peace and joy when the enemy is defeated.

As in the opening of the musical, it is quite true that the Ozians felt joyful when they heard about the Witch's death in just the same way that we, as observers of the 1939 movie, celebrated with Dorothy and her friends when the Witch melted into oblivion. But Girard and many of today's cultural theorists are beginning to wonder if there is more to the story than that. They wonder if the celebration is concealing a deeper truth that would be revealed if we could hear the story of the villain. If the winners allowed themselves to actually hear the villain's story, the peace and joy they achieved through his defeat might evaporate into remorse and guilt.

Let's look at a fairy tale and imagine what we might hear if the villain told us his or her story. Take Hansel and Gretel, for instance, the fairy tale of two children who get lost in a wood and become the prisoners of a wicked old witch. Is there any reason you can think of why an old woman would be living alone in the woods longing for the company of children? Perhaps she is a childless widow or a woman who longed to be a mother but never had children. Or maybe she lost her children to sickness or the maw of a wild animal. What if, when she told us her version, we learned that the children weren't locked up as prisoners, but to prevent animals from stealing them away, as happened to her own children? How happy would we feel at the end of the story when the woman is roasted in her own oven, perhaps an oven she was heating to prepare a special meal for the children? Would we celebrate her death? And might we then be able to focus on the truly wicked people in this story, the stepmother who wants to be rid of her stepchildren and the father who does not stand up to her?

Once you begin to imagine yourself inside the minds and hearts of the ogres, witches and monsters of fairy tales you can create all kinds of stories that might explain their behavior in an innocent way. Rather than being totally evil beings bent on destruction, they become sad, lonely people whose motives and actions are so misunderstood that the community comes to believe in the necessity of their death. This is what happened to Gregory Maguire, the author of the novel that inspired *Wicked*, the musical.

In his novel *Wicked: The Life and Times of the Wicked Witch of the West*, Gregory Maguire wrestles with the question of evil. Maguire describes how he began the novel. In 1990, in London for the build-up to the first Iraq war, he "became riveted by how the British press vilified Saddam

Hussein to galvanize public opinion in support of the war."[3] Maguire describes himself as "a progressive liberal" who, under the influence of the press attacks against Hussein, found that his "politics had shifted way to the right."[4] His transformation into an advocate for war, any war, shocked him. "How," he asked himself, "did I lose my moorings so quickly?"[5]

As a writer, Maguire was not afraid to explore the dark places of the human soul. He decided to explore the problem of evil in his next novel. He wanted to know how someone like Saddam could become the abhorrent human being that he so obviously was, and examine how he, Maguire, could slide into the same evil place with so little provocation. He chose as his vehicle a familiar childhood story about wickedness, using the Wicked Witch as his stand-in for Saddam, and set out to explore exactly how the Wicked Witch became so evil in the first place. What he found out was that no matter how hard he tried to write wickedness into the character of the Witch, whom he named Elphaba, she refused to comply. She seemed to be struggling with him to tell her own story. Though he began his writing project with hatred for his main character, he realized he was beginning to have compassion for her. Rather than a paragon of wickedness, he realized that Elphaba was a lonely little girl, with an unfortunate birth defect: green skin. Unloved by her father and ostracized by her community, she was a sad, emotionally scarred victim who wanted only to tell her story and be accepted.

What a remarkable reversal – from paragon of evil to a victim of persecution. Girard explains that this is exactly the reversal that the persecutors (the Heroes of fairy tales and myths) want to avoid, and do so by telling of their glorious triumph excluding the point of view of the victim (the Villain). He explains that if persecutors succeed in "reducing [the victim] to silence, the persecutors' belief in the [the victim's] guilt would have been unanimous... This belief would have prevailed so totally that every future account of the affair would have been given by people sharing it... The accusations would be so powerful that they would be raised to the status of truth."[6] With the victim silenced and his version of what happened lost, often because he has been killed, there is no one to challenge the victor's story. The incomplete and distorted story rises to the level of truth, and a Myth is born.

But surely not all villains are misunderstood victims. Don't evil people really exist? What would have happened if Maguire tried the same exercise with Saddam himself, a real life bad guy, instead of the fictitious Wicked Witch? All those good guy/bad guy movies aren't completely make believe – after all, amoral villains who want to destroy the world with all manner of apocalyptic violence are not figments of Hollywood's imagination. We've witnessed more than enough proof throughout the twentieth century of such evil: the cruel destruction of life on September 11, the genocide of the Jews by Hitler, the murders and imprisonment of the millions who opposed Stalin, Saddam's ruthless extermination of his perceived enemies. These examples suffice to point out that people do exist who commit remorseless acts of evil, regardless of our clever retelling of the fairy tales.

Yes, evil exists. That point is indisputable. The vital question that is raised by retelling and reexamining fairy tales, and which is addressed expertly and artistically in the musical, ***Wicked***, is this: How do we tell the difference between the truly evil and the misunderstood victim? As our exercise with Hansel and Gretel has shown us, evil is sometimes harder to identify than appears at first glance. Is it possible that we might be mistaken in our accusations? Once we find evil we feel justified in taking some pretty extreme measures to root it out. We might shove the evil one in an oven, or drop a house on them, or launch a war to annihilate them from the face of the earth. But what happens if we made a mistake? Before we do any of these things, might it be wise to be absolutely certain that our accusations of evil are true?

As we delve deeper into these issues, no doubt examples spring to mind of times when we as a nation made mistakes in our judgment of evil. During World War II, all Americans of Japanese decent were locked into concentration camps out of fear that all Japanese were the enemy. In college, I had a professor who was born in such a camp. Although his family was a threat to no one, there he was – an innocent young child charged, tried and convicted of treasonous intentions by virtue of his genetics alone. As a nation, we regret these actions, and have even apologized for them. This is a good example of how absolute certainty about evil can crumble into dust.

SATAN
THE ACCUSER

In the Bible, the Hebrew word for Satan can be translated to mean either Adversary or Accuser. These meanings give us insight into the nature of Satanic evil. It is adversarial, because it thrives on sowing and enflaming conflict in human communities, and it does this through the unusual mechanism of false accusation. It seems that Satan is another name for the art of deflecting blame from oneself onto others.

Practitioners of this art are everywhere. When someone gets caught with his hand in the proverbial cookie jar, all too often he points the finger at someone who happened to be standing nearby, falsely accusing them of the crime. Our courts exist to weed out these false accusations from the truth. During political campaigns we find the example of negative campaign advertising, which is nothing more than an avalanche of false accusations designed to protect candidates from having to disclose their positions on real campaign issues. When everyone is busy pointing a finger rather than accepting responsibility, you can be sure that the Biblical Satan is at work.

Biblical wisdom suggests that to locate evil, we look for the source of the accusation. The uncomfortable truth may be that the accuser, and not the accused, is the one doing Satan's work.

The lynching of black men in the South in the decades after the Civil War is another sad example. Lynching statistics were kept between 1882 and 1968. During those 86 years 4,743 victims were murdered, 3,500 of them African Americans. Most sociologists today agree that these 3,500 murders were racially motivated. As if such callous cruelty to the victim and his family were not enough, many of those who gathered to witness the lynching took photographs of the hanging victim as if they were at a circus. Many of those photographs were made into postcards and distributed to family and friends as a gruesome record of the event.[7] Those photographs and postcards are a silent witness to the murderers' inability to see the evil in their own deeds and the innocence of their victims.

So we find in this extraordinary musical, inspired by the Maguire novel, the same story found in the 1939 movie, but told from the perspective of someone who has been wrongly accused of evil. The original movie tells the story of what happened in Oz during the last days of the Wizard's reign from the point of view of Dorothy and her friends. They are the heroes, the victors in the battle against the Witch. This is the version that we can now identify as a Myth because the Wicked Witch's version never gets told. The stage musical, on the other hand, tells the story of the same time period but from the point of view of the loser of the battle. *Wicked* tells the story of the one who was killed from her perspective, in her voice. This is the perspective that the Myth wants to conceal.

As we journey through the events of the musical, daring to listen to the Witch's story, we will learn things that Dorothy and her friends couldn't bear to hear. The truth is that Dorothy, the Tin Man, the Cowardly Lion and the Scarecrow are good people just like you and me. Is it possible that good people could do something so bad as to kill an innocent person? Is it really good news that the Wicked Witch is dead?

3

Good News! She's Dead!

The persecutors... believe they have on their hands a dangerous person, someone evil, of whom they must rid the community. What could be more sincere than their hatred?

RENÉ GIRARD,
I See Satan Fall Like Lightning

That is all myth is – an absolute faith in the victim's total power of evil that liberates the persecutors from reciprocal recriminations and, therefore, is identical with an absolute faith in the total power of good.

RENÉ GIRARD,
Job: The Victim of His People

Sometimes I think that vengeance is habit forming too.
A stiffness of attitude.

MAGUIRE, *Wicked*

Wicked opens with a proclamation of faith in the absolute difference between good and evil, a hallmark of Myth telling. But unlike Myths, which end with the forces of evil getting trounced by the power of good, *Wicked* reverses the order and begins with the death of the enemy. If *Wicked* were just another Myth, like so many fairy tales or action adventures, the play would end in the opening minutes – there would be nothing left to say. The celebration would wind down, the Ozians would go home spent and exhilarated, their faith in the power of good restored, and that would be the end of the story. But the opening celebration signals that we're going to hear a story unlike any we have heard before. It's as if the show's creators are saying to the audience, "Brace yourselves, ladies and gentlemen, because you're not in Kansas anymore!"

In fact, that opening scene is so insightful and anti-Mythological, that the first time I saw it I found myself wondering if Stephen Schwartz and Winnie Holzman, the composer and writer of the show, were familiar with Girard's work. By the end of the musical, I wouldn't have been surprised to find out that they had intentionally set about putting Girard's ideas to music. That was not their intention, of course, but Girard began as a professor of literature and it was through studying the great writers of the past that he developed his ideas. Excellent storytellers are keen observers of human conflict who describe in their works of fiction the workings of the real world. Using imaginary people, plots and landscapes, they offer profound insights into the way you and I interact in our communities, often challenging our views of morality, right and wrong. Schwartz and Holzman belong to that great tradition of writers who illuminate the truth that is concealed by Myth.

As we explore the musical, you may feel as stunned as Dorothy and her friends when Toto pulled back the curtain on the Wizard's illusion-making apparatus. Lies told by the Myth will be exposed and the beliefs that have gone unquestioned within it will be dismantled. To begin, the musical poses the most difficult question of all: Why do we believe in Myths? Girard's main theory is that Myths are stories told that conceal a terrible wrong, an act of persecution that often ends in murder. He thinks Mythological thinking is everywhere – not just in fairy tales and movies, but that it exists as part of the fabric of our communities. But if Myths are really terrible lies, why do we believe in them? We can also ask that question in the words of the musical: When is it good news that someone is dead?

The Ozians sing the opening lyric as if the answer is so obvious that the question need not be asked. Someone's death is good news when they are wicked, of course, when our lives are threatened and their death will restore peace. This is the central promise of the Myth and one that seems to be true: Peace can be achieved or restored by finding and destroying the threat to that peace. We see this belief expressed daily in actions throughout the world that are intended to combat terrorism. Terrorists threaten the peace with violence and wanton disregard for human life. To protect the peace and innocent lives, these terrorists must be identified and destroyed. Above all else, the Myth promises a straightforward formula to reach peace through such destruction.

The Myth doesn't just promise peace – it comes complete with a strategy to achieve it. The title of the opening song, "No One Mourns the Wicked," hints at part of that strategy while the song itself tells us much of how it works. As we progress through the musical, we will observe three more elements of this strategy, identified as Mythological Rules to indicate that they comprise something like a recipe for peace. Mythological Rule #1 is found in the opening song, and states: *Evil can and must be identified with absolute certainty.*

Wicked's composer, Stephen Schwartz, related: "I hardly ever start by composing the opening number, but this is the song I started writing first. I wanted to open with everyone celebrating, a sort of 'Ding Dong the Witch is Dead' for the Wicked Witch of the West. It's rhythmic and explosive, but somewhat discordant to our ears."[1] Schwartz begins the show where Myth ends, with his version of the celebration of the death of a witch. He starts his show with the celebration in Munchkinland of the death of the Witch of the East by the plummeting house that is our introduction to the Land of Oz in the 1939 movie. By his own admission, his version is nothing like the sweet, childlike ditty sung by the Munchkins. Here, again are the opening words of the musical:

Good News!
She's Dead!
The Witch of the West is dead!
The Wickedest Witch there ever was
The enemy of all of us here in Oz
Is dead!
Good News!
Good News!

If we read the lyrics without listening to the music, the words suggest that the Ozians are as confident as the Munchkins were that wickedness has been identified and destroyed. They appear to be dwelling securely within the Myth, proclaiming their adherence to Rule #1 – not only do they believe that evil can be identified with absolute certainty, they have the tangible proof in their own feelings of relief and restored calm. They are now free to celebrate a return to their peaceful and tranquil lives, which had been threatened by the Witch. But there are hints even in these opening moments that their faith is not justified. The discordant minor key, which is often used to express distress, as well as the characters' "explosive" way of singing, function like the many hints in Baum's novel, forcing us to question what the lyrics proclaim – was the Witch's death a cause for celebration? Perhaps the good news about the restoration of peace is not as good as the Ozians think it is.

After these few verses, Glinda the Good Witch arrives in a magic bubble to the joy of the crowd. She quickly joins the celebration, a sparkling antidote to the minor key of the chorus, assuring everyone that they have reason to celebrate. She sings:

Let us be glad
Let us be grateful
Let us rejoicify that goodness could subdue
The wicked workings of you-know-who
Isn't it nice to know
That good will conquer evil?

The truth we all believe'll by and by
Outlive a lie
For you and—

She sings her agreement that happy endings are possible, something the Ozian chorus apparently needs to hear. Despite their bold words, their faith in Rule #1 needs bolstering, so Glinda obliges by singing, "Isn't it nice to know that good will conquer evil?" Again, we recognize this as one of the elements of Myth – not only are good and evil easy to identify, but good always wins in the end. We are left to wonder about this obvious need for reassurance from Glinda – could the Ozians be feeling a little bit guilty about their feelings of joy at someone's death, even the death of a witch?

Glinda's next line contains the words "truth" and "lie." She sings that this belief in good conquering evil is a truth that has the power to "outlive a lie." Knowing what we know now about Myth, and having been duly warned by a critical reading of Baum's novel, this language of truth and lie demands our attention. What lie is Glinda referring to? To answer that, we need to take a moment to situate ourselves in the plot of the show.

The show opens with the death of the Witch of the West, but the rest of the show until the closing scene is told in flashback. Through the action, dialogue and songs of the production, we are given the details of the events that led up to this death and the reason why it is a cause for celebration. Our narrator for this back story is Glinda. And who is Glinda? What does she represent as she rides in on her magic bubble full of the reassurances the Ozians need to hear?

In these opening moments, Glinda is dutifully performing her role as mouthpiece of the government of Oz. The "truth" she is singing about, of good conquering evil, is actually the lie of all Myths that the complete story has been told, that evil has been identified without a doubt. The "lie" Glinda sings about is none other than what Girard has identified as the hiding or distorting of the perspective of the victim, which in this case would be the version of events that the Witch would tell. The truth we all know and believe is the Mythological version of the Witch's death told by Glinda who, as the voice of Myth, is confident that it will outlive the "lie" told by victims who proclaim their innocence.

Though Glinda is giving voice to the Myth, it is actually her role in the show to deliver the Witch's perspective, thus revealing the truth Myth relies on keeping hidden. As in the Baum novel, a character says one thing yet does another. Let's see how this simultaneous proclamation and unmasking of the Myth unfolds.

After Glinda reassures everyone that the Witch is really dead, the Ozians continue with their song. Listen to the reasons they offer for why they are celebrating the death of the Witch of the West:

OZIAN:
No one mourns the wicked

OZIAN:
No one cries: "They won't return!"

OZIANS:
No one lays a lily on their grave

OZIAN MAN:
The good man scorns the wicked!

WOMEN:
Through their lives our children learn:

OZIANS:
What we miss
When we misbehave ...

GLINDA:
And goodness knows
The wicked's lives are lonely
Goodness knows
The wicked die alone

It just shows when you're wicked
You're left only
On your own ...

OZIANS:
Yes, goodness knows
The wicked's lives are lonely
Goodness knows
The wicked cry alone
Nothing grows for the wicked
They reap only
What they've sown ...

They are offering a repetition of Rule #1, of easily identifiable good and evil. How do they know if someone is evil? It has very little to do with the behavior of the wicked person and everything to do with how the "good" people react to her. Someone is wicked if no one mourns their death or lays a lily on their grave or wants to be like them when they grow up. Someone is wicked if they are lonely and die alone. Rather than offering us a list of all the terrible things the witch has done to them, they offer us insight into their own fears of loneliness and rejection by their family and friends. It seems that someone is wicked if everyone agrees that they are.

Let's look a little more closely at the beliefs of the Ozians. We can list three beliefs that are an implicit part of Rule #1 and appear to be behind the reason that the Witch's death can be celebrated. The first assumption is that evil exists somewhere out there – outside our community – and it wants nothing more than our community's destruction. The second assumption is that we have the right and responsibility to destroy that evil before it can destroy us. Once we have done that, of course, we will be safe once again. Peace and joy will be ours. So, to state it briefly:

Assumptions Behind Rule #1:

- Evil is somewhere outside our community.
- have the right and responsibility to destroy it.
- ly then will we have peace.

These assumptions give us a formula for peace. They justify the use of violence in certain circumstances: to rid our communities of the evil that threatens peace. The formula demands, however, that we be able to identify the evil, find it with absolute certainty and, with equal decisiveness, destroy it. In fact, the restoration of peace seems to hinge more on the confidence everyone has in their accusations of evil than in whether their accusations are true. To test this, we might wonder what would happen if there were some doubt about the accusation. What would happen to the celebration and the promise of peace if the Ozians' faith in the wickedness of the Witch wavered?

We are about to find out because, as the story demonstrates, the Ozians are not quite sure they buy into the Mythological version of events. They have a few questions for Glinda before she flies away in her sparkly bubble. A lone Ozian asks the question that launches the musical, the question that sends the audience on a topsy-turvy, upside-down look at the classical, movie version of this fairy tale. The Ozian asks, "Glinda, why does wickedness happen?" Glinda responds with another question, "Are people born wicked, or do they have wickedness thrust upon them?"

Glinda's question gives voice to the unspoken worry of the Ozians that there has been some mistake. Was the Witch truly wicked or might there have been extenuating circumstances that could explain her behavior? Worst of all, was there something we, the Ozians, did that "thrust" wickedness upon her?

Glinda answers these questions by telling the Witch's story on her behalf. But this is the one thing that weakens the strength of the Myth and is therefore taboo within the Mythological world – we must never, ever give the victim a voice. The audience is treated to a scene that reveals the circumstances of the Witch's birth. Her mother is seduced by a stranger who plies her with a green elixir then leaves town. Not only is the Witch a bastard child, she bears an unfortunate mark of her illegitimacy: She is born green.

Glinda explains, "So you see, it couldn't have been easy." But the Ozians, after asking the question, seem intent on ignoring what they have just learned. They sing again, louder and more determined than ever, that the Witch's death was good news.

ALL:
Now at last, there's joy throughout the land
And
Goodness knows
We know what goodness is
Goodness knows
The wicked die alone
Woe to those
Who spurn what goodnesses
They are shown
No one mourns the wicked

GLINDA:
Good News!

CROWD:
No one mourns the wicked

GLINDA:
Good News!

ALL:
No one mourns the wicked!
Wicked!
Wicked!

They want to believe with all their hearts that they can tell the difference between goodness and wickedness, that there is no doubt about the morality of their celebration. At this first hint that something has been hidden from their view, the Ozians retreat into their belief that they are undeniably good. They aren't ready yet to have their confidence in their own motives shaken to the core.

Why is it so hard for the Ozians to face their own fallibility? Could the Ozians be wicked themselves, perhaps even more evil than the

FIT FOR COMBAT

My father tells a story of what happened when he was inducted into the army during World War II. It was a time in our nation's history when we felt quite sure who was our enemy, and we trained our young men to kill them on the battlefields of war. As part of his psychological evaluation, my father was asked if he was willing to kill someone – presumably a German or Japanese soldier. He answered, "Not if I could see his face." My father says that the examiner was shocked by his answer and appeared to doubt his fitness for combat.

Luckily the war ended before my dad had to make the difficult decision of whether or not to kill another human being, but he expressed very well the moral dilemma facing all soldiers. As part of their training, soldiers are taught to objectify and demonize their enemy while regarding their own efforts as virtuous and patriotic. They are taught that they and their enemies have nothing whatever in common, especially not decency or truth or honor. How hard it is to believe this when confronted face to face with another human being. My father's fear was that despite his training, if he were ever to gaze into the eyes of his enemy, he would see a fellow soldier not unlike himself with a family and dreams for the future. If he hesitated, he or a comrade could be killed. And if he did kill, he would never be able to celebrate his actions.

Unable to believe in the absolute evil of his enemy, my father dwelled outside the Myth where there are no easy answers and no quick remedies.

Witch in their willingness to overlook their complicity in the death of a potentially innocent person? If that were so, if we could detach the accusation of evil from the Witch and pin it on the Ozians, we would still be playing within the rules of the Myth. It would still be an exercise in finding evil with absolute certainty. Our fingers are still pointing, but now the direction has changed and it matters little to the peace we will feel if this time we've gotten it right. No, the answer is not so simple. No answer outside the Myth is. One of the hallmarks of Myth is its black and white certainty about things. When you are one hundred percent, absolutely sure you have located evil, it may be that you are locked securely within the Myth.

No, the Ozians are no more wicked or evil than you and I. Their retreat away from the truth and back inside the lies of the Myth is completely understandable, perhaps even justified because the Myth has a way of delivering on its promise of peace. If you follow the rules, beginning with #1, the chances are good that your community will achieve a sense of peace. It may be fleeting, and it may require more and more applications of the Mythological Rules, but once begun a measure of peace is guaranteed.

Like the Ozians, families will unite in celebration and strangers will become friends in the joyous moments of relief after the identified threat has been eliminated. Even if the threat were imaginary, once it is removed we all feel better. When Americans locked up Japanese-Americans during World War II, they felt more secure even if though that security was only an illusion. When whites lynched black men in the South, they felt a sense of unity and community inspired and created by their violent activities. By eliminating the perceived threat to their safety and the security of their communities, these men gained identity through a common purpose. The Mythological formula for peace is at once effective and diabolical. It delivers peace and conceals the cost in one brilliant maneuver by assuring us that evil can be located and eliminated from our communities, without personal consequence.

It is easy to see how this Myth is exhibited in our daily lives and communities. Think of office life, for example. Departments may define themselves relative to each other by reinforcing beliefs such as,

"We in Personnel are so much more efficient than the IT Department." Or small groups within the Personnel Department may unite in water cooler gossip against their boss or team leader to feel a sense of camaraderie. A common focus for gossip or outright hatred conceals any disagreement that might arise between the members of the group itself. As long as the team leader is being scapegoated, the members of the team are best friends. This dynamic operates for any group of any size, no matter how it defines itself – a political party, a religious community, a social action group, a sorority, a school, a family, a club, or a clique. All are at risk of falling into this destructive way of achieving peace if the bond that brought them together is too weak to withstand the petty quarreling and resentment that inevitably results when human beings live and work together.

Let's look at another example – the legendary feud between the "Hatfields and McCoys." They were two hillbilly families with porch-sitting grandmas and tobacco-chewing, gun-toting men, who spent their spare time hunting down men in the other family. The families were enemies, for sure, but strangely, no one could say why. Not being able to say why didn't seem to matter much. What mattered was that hating the McCoys defined you as a Hatfield, and vice versa.

If we could go back to the origin of the feud, we might find out, for instance that, Mr. McCoy did steal somebody's chickens and so is guilty of a crime. But that really doesn't matter, because the Hatfields are not pursuing the entire McCoy clan in order to punish Mr. McCoy for stealing. The old coot is long dead, anyway. What they are doing through their shared hatred is creating a sense of community and family identity. Rather than face the problems within their family, it is easier for the Hatfields to hate the McCoys and achieve unity by focusing on an enemy. In this way, the McCoys are scapegoats for the Hatfields. Mr. McCoy, though a chicken thief, is not guilty of the petty hatred and resentments within the Hatfield family that are resolved on the cheap by their unifying hatred.

It is important to understand that within the Myth told about good and evil the distinction between true guilt and false guilt is not made. Whether one is truly guilty of the crime of chicken theft or not is irrelevant to the Myth, so both the truly guilty and the truly innocent end up in the same category. A true rapist and a falsely accused rapist can both hang from the same tree and within the Myth there is no difference between them. Because they both serve to cleanse the community of its own conflict, within the Myth they are treated as if they were identical.

As Galinda will sing to Elphaba not very long from now, "It's not about aptitude, it's the way you're viewed/So it's very shrewd to be, very very popular like me!" Galinda understands the workings of the Myth all too well. She knows it is deliberately blind to true distinctions of good and evil in order to use those labels for its own purposes: to find scapegoats. The Myth deliberately blinds us so that we will not seek to make a distinction where the Myth claims there is none.

When the Ozians sing that the Witch is wicked by definition, they know that they are not. It is goodness (themselves) that will conquer evil (Elphaba). The Ozians have formed their sense of community on the cheap by sacrificing Elphaba to their needs. That is, rather than face their own wickedness – daily failure to express love, hurtful patterns of gossip and blaming, resentments, fits of anger – they surrender all responsibility for these actions by projecting onto Elphaba their own hurtful experiences. And in the process they generate a fabulous cathartic effect, like the joyful thrill experienced after throat-straining cheering for sporting victories. Where once there were petty quarrels and disharmony, all has been transformed into joy, peace and celebration.

The promise of peace is seductive. In *Wicked*, as in Baum's novel, this promise is symbolized by the Emerald City, the one place where all your dreams come true. Who wouldn't want to live in such a tranquil city ruled by a beneficent Wizard? And because the promise is so seductive, the Ozians have not wanted to upset the apple cart by asking too many questions. Peace is such a valuable commodity – communities simply cannot survive without it in some form – that the Myth is betting that we won't care exactly how the peace is achieved, as long as we are secure. It is easier for the Ozians to maintain the illusion of the Wonderful Wizard than to question how he got there. But the Wizard's words to Dorothy from Baum's novel are haunting: Is it true that both Oz and our world are places where "everyone must pay for everything he gets"?

But surely we don't need *Wicked* to tell us that peace costs and much sacrifice is required for its maintenance. This country has sacrificed many times in our history, and is doing so today: fighting wars with bravery and honor. But is there more to the promise of peace than that – something we haven't thought about yet? What if the peace of Oz comes with a price that actually threatens the peace rather than guarantees it?

Delving into the ideas of *Wicked* is a little like taking out our reading glasses to look intently at the fine print on the last page of a long contract. The Myth has a deal for us and it hawks it like a real showman: "Get your peace here! Today only get bargain basement prices! Just sign on the dotted line and the peace is yours!" The musical is not going to tell us what to do – whether to sign or not is our decision. But it will give us a chance to read the fine print and become completely knowledgeable about the terms of the contract. Then we can decide if we like the terms enough to take the deal. Perhaps instead of signing, we will begin to look around for other peace vendors, ones that offer us terms we can live with.

Someone in that crowd of Ozians is not yet ready to sign. Before Glinda leaves, he calls out one last question: "Glinda! Is it true – you were her friend?!" The very question elicits gasps from the Ozians. What if Glinda, the Good, was a friend of this Wicked Witch? Because they are still dwelling deep within the Myth, the Ozians can interpret the possibility of such a friendship in only one of two ways: Either Glinda is not as good as she appears, or the Witch was not truly wicked. Within the Myth there are no grey areas; there is no room for good people who sometimes do bad things or bad people who are capable of good. As Girard has written:

> "The well-oiled ... mechanism [of Myth] generates an absolutely 'perfect' world ... There is no room in this world for unpunished injustice or unsanctioned evil, any more than there is a place for the just person who is unlucky or the persecuted person who is innocent."[2]

Within the Myth, if Glinda answers yes, if she was the witch's friend, the Ozians will be forced to doubt her goodness, as well as their own. If Glinda is not as good as they think she is or, even worse, the Witch was not truly wicked, they have no right to celebrate her death. The lyric, "Good News!" may be more heartless than they are ready to admit. And tragically, the peace they long for may still remain out of reach. If what they fear about Glinda and the Witch is true, they will urgently need to know the answer to the most vital question of all: How can good people make their world safe if they cannot celebrate the death of a wicked witch?

Making Good – And Evil

Learning to love yourself / It is the greatest love of all.

LINDA CREED and MICHAEL MASSER,
Greatest Love of All

He who fights with monsters might take care lest he thereby become a monster.

FREIDRICH NIETZSCHE,
Beyond Good and Evil

The musical is now well underway and the question that dominates the next few scenes is whether there is any difference at all between what we call good and what we call evil. Schwartz and Holzman lead us into a hall of mirrors in which distinctions are distorted and warped so completely that all differences are erased.

Let's look at what happens as we meet the Wicked Witch for the first time. The scene is the first day of school at Shiz University, and students are bustling here and there when the Witch enters the scene. It is easy to tell who she is, because she is the only green-skinned person present.

Imagine what it would be like to be green, to be judged before you could utter a word. Even before you could tell someone your name, they had already decided that they knew who you were. Perhaps it is not that hard to imagine. Perhaps you bear a distinguishing mark, an outward sign of your difference, and are familiar with the dynamic of being pre-judged.

We often talk about it more benignly as "first impressions." I know I was told to be sure I always made a "good" first impression, especially on job interviews. Apparently the right clothes, the proper posture, a firm handshake and confident smile were my armor to protect myself from leaving a "bad" impression on others. I learned that once an impression was formed, especially a bad one, it was nearly impossible to reverse.

However, on her first day at her new school, Elphaba cannot rely on her clothes, posture, or facial expressions. All she can do is stand there in all her striking greenness, helpless to prevent a negative impression from falling with a thud into the hearts and minds of her fellow students. Each time she meets someone new she can rely on that person to judge her with the certainty of a force of nature, with the reliability of gravity. Her only defense is to face their prejudice head on with a false bravado, a cynical sarcasm that conceals her pain. "What?" she says to the silent, gaping crowd of new students. "What are you looking at? Oh, do I have something in my teeth? Okay, let's get this over with. No, I'm not seasick. Yes, I've always been green. No, I didn't chew grass as a child."

The Witch has arrived with her sister and her father, Frex. Upon hearing these first remarks by his daughter, Frex rebukes her. It is the first time we hear the Witch's name and it is spoken in anger. Elphaba accepts her father's rebuke as her introduction to the other students and then introduces her sister.

ELPHABA:
Oh, this is my younger sister, Nessarose. As you can see, she is a perfectly normal color.

FREX:
Elphaba, stop making a spectacle of yourself! I'm only sending you here for one reason ...

ELPHABA:
Yes, I know, to look after Nessarose.

We quickly learn that Elphaba is not here as a student, but as a caretaker for her sister, the wheelchair-bound Nessarose. Frex's favoritism toward Nessarose becomes painfully obvious when he presents Nessa with a gift – a pair of jeweled silver shoes. For some unknown reason, though Elphaba is the older sister, it is Nessarose who is heir to her father and will become the Governor of Munchkinland when he dies.

Though one sister has won her father's approval and the other has not, both sisters bear distinguishing outward signs that mark them as unusual. Although Nessarose cannot walk, it is only Elphaba's strange skin color that repels her father's affection, attracts unwelcome attention and leaves bad impressions among her peers. We could explain this away by saying that people in wheelchairs are not an uncommon sight, while green skin is, but I think that would do a disservice to the ideas at work in the musical. Remember, we are in Oz not "Kansas." As far as we know, Nessarose is the only person in Oz who cannot walk, while Elphaba's greenness may not be a strange phenomenon at all. After all, there is an entire city of green, the Emerald City, which is the capital of the country.

So we have two marks – one that confers love and prestige and future honor, and the other which deflects love and promises ostracism and loneliness. The marks themselves do not inherently confer such qualities. It seems completely arbitrary which mark implies glory and which condemnation. In fact, one can easily imagine how Elphaba's greenness could be perceived as a sign of honor – she is the color of power, the color of the Emerald City. But this is not the case. Here we have the first suggestion from the authors about the arbitrary nature of good and evil in the Land of Oz – people are not born wicked but rather have the designation of wickedness thrust upon them.

Next, we are led on a seesaw adventure as we try to determine who is good and who is wicked. When Glinda enters the scene, she is not "Glinda" but "Galinda," a young college student in a time before she becomes a government official. She is clearly popular from the start, as she enters the stage surrounded by cloying admirers, while Elphaba stands alone, isolated by her strange skin color. It is clear at this very first meeting that Galinda is riding high, socially superior and Elphaba is an outcast, shunned by everyone she meets. If this were a contest, we would say that at this point Galinda has the upper hand.

Now we meet the Headmistress of the school, Madame Morrible, who has the power to hand-select the students in the most sought after class at the university, taught by Madame Morrible herself. Each year, she teaches the class only if she finds a worthy student, and she soon realizes that Elphaba possesses magical powers. Elphaba's rare talent could someday lead to a meeting with the Wizard and an appointment in the government of Oz. Immediately, Morrible invites Elphaba to be her only student this semester. Galinda, who wants nothing more than to be come a sorceress herself, is refused entry to the coveted sorcery class. In the blink of an eye, Elphaba is now up and Galinda is down.

It is at this moment, when Elphaba has received recognition from someone in power, perhaps for the first time in her life, that she reveals her feelings in a poignant solo. Though the world has been cruel to Elphaba and rejected her so consistently, she wants with all her heart to be accepted and recognized for who she is. Not as a strange, green girl, but as a person with gifts and abilities who has something of value to offer. From her outsider status, Elphaba studied the workings of the world and she learned one thing for sure – the surest way to acceptance is association with someone in power. Elphaba realized that rubbing shoulders with those in high esteem created a contagion of admiration. She saw it when Madame Morrible lavished attention on Nessarose because she was her father's favorite. Now she experienced this contagion herself as Morrible's invitation to the sorcery class caused Galinda – the most popular girl in all the school – to be jealous of her! What further envy and admiration might she incur if the Wizard, the most powerful and adored man in the land, accepted her?

In her song, Elphaba imagines what it will be like to meet the Wizard. Unlike the rest of the world, she believes he will see past her greenness to who she truly is, someone on whom he can rely. His

POPULAR BY ASSOCIATION

I attended an all girls' Catholic high school where we wore plaid uniforms and saddle shoes. We were boy crazy, had crushes on our male teachers, and engaged in the typical cliquey behavior of all high school girls. There was an "in" crowd and an "out" crowd and you may have already guessed that I was definitely out. I didn't sneak cigarettes, nor did I roll my uniform skirt to mini-skirt length on the way to school. I studied hard and did my homework and was a general nerd. There were a few weeks, though, when I had visions of climbing to the pinnacle of the pecking order.

We were assigned to work in groups on a history project and one of the popular girls asked me to be part of her group. I was thrilled! It didn't occur to me right away that it was a ploy on her part to get a good grade on the project. She figured – rightly – that I would do all the work and our teacher would be more inclined to give the group a good grade if I were in it. For a while, though, I enjoyed being chosen to associate with someone of her high popularity quotient. It was fun being cool, even though it wasn't real and it couldn't last.

Young and old alike try to "catch" coolness from someone already anointed, often by imitating popular sports or entertainment figures. We wear the clothes, listen to the music, drive the car, and live in the neighborhoods of those we admire, so we can catch some of their cool. Luckily, I realized that my classmate was manipulating me, so I did not begin to smoke or roll my skirt in imitation of her. But when we submit to the influence of others in order to acquire some quality they seem to possess, we lose ourselves, becoming instead cookie-cutter images of one another rather than truly who we are.

authority will force a reinterpretation of what it means to be green. She tells us:

Once I'm with the Wizard
My whole life will change
'Cuz once you're with the Wizard
No one thinks you're strange
No father is not proud of you
No sister acts ashamed
And all of Oz has to love you
When by the Wizard, you're acclaimed

Unfortunately, Elphaba believes in the rules of how to gain acceptance and love, and she is committed to following them with a vengeance. She accepts the Ozian view that being green is not a good thing at all. She wants to find a way to "make good," as she tells us in her song, and end her exile once and for all. When she is accepted by the Wizard she believes she will be catapulted from the down side of the see-saw to the upside so fast and hard that she may fly up into the sky and no one will be able to bring her down again. And just in case, as a sort of insurance policy, she will allow the Wizard to "degreenify" her. In her song, she imagines exactly what the Wizard will say:

And one day, he'll say to me: "Elphaba,
A girl who is so superior
Shouldn't a girl who's so good inside
Have a matching exterior?
And since folks here to an absurd degree
Seem fixated on your verdigris
Would it be all right by you
If I de-greenify you?"

She hesitates briefly, pretending that whether or not she is green is "not important" to her, but she quickly agrees. There will be no more green Elphaba. No more distinguishing mark that caused all the bad impressions to stick to her like glue. She will be sponged clean and she's delighted.

Then she has a vision about a day when "there'll be a celebration throughout Oz that's all to do with me!" The audience has already been to that celebration – it's how the show opened. We have seen the end of the story for Elphaba. We know that this playing by the rules will lead to her death and that all of Oz will be rejoicing in it. If we could warn her, we would. *Don't go to Morrible's sorcery class, Elphaba. Don't try to be accepted. Don't stop being green.* But it's too late. Elphaba is launched on a path to erase the sign of her difference and truthfully, we understand her desire to be accepted. It is our desire, too.

So far, we have been following the up-down seesaw of Galinda and Elphaba's relationship. The ride continues with a marvelous duet called, "What is This Feeling?" As they sing, the audience sees the outcome of their attempts to one-up each other – Galinda and Elphaba become identical! By the end of this song, what was a tiny smudge on the Ozian's ability to distinguish good from evil has become a grimy, sooty haze that no one will be able to see through.

The song opens with Galinda and Elphaba occupying opposite corners of the stage, each standing in a spotlight and occupied with writing a letter home. They confess to being upset about the roommate situation at Shiz. When Madame Morrible turned their world upside-down by denying Galinda admission to the sorcery class and allowing Elphaba in, she also assigned them to be roommates. Neither one was happy about it but now we find out that they are more than unhappy. They sing either in unison (no differences) or in alternating phrases (up-down, down-up) about an overpowering feeling:

BOTH:
Yes, there's been some confusion
For you see my roommate is …

GALINDA:
Unusually, and exceedingly peculiar
And altogether quite impossible to describe …

ELPHABA:
Blonde.

GALINDA:
What is this feeling
So sudden and new?

ELPHABA:
I felt the moment
I laid eyes on you ...

GALINDA:
My pulse is rushing ...

ELPHABA:
My head is reeling ...

GALINDA:
My face is flushing ...

BOTH:
What is this feeling?
Fervid as a flame
Does it have a name?
Yes!
Loathing
Unadulterated loathing ...

GALINDA:
For your face ...

ELPHABA:
Your voice ...

GALINDA:
Your clothing ...

BOTH:
Let's just say – I loathe it all!
Ev'ry little trait, however small
Makes my very flesh begin to crawl
With simple utter loathing
There's a strange exhilaration
In such total detestation
It's so pure! So strong!
Though I do admit it came on fast
Still I do believe that it can last
And I will be loathing
Loathing you
My whole life long!

Of course, the irony is not lost on the audience. Elphaba is judging Galinda for being blonde in the same way that Galinda, and everyone else, judges Elphaba for being green. In their contempt for each other, they are desperately trying to prove how completely different they are from one another. The song can be summed up this way: She's the bad one, not me – I'm good! If someone had interrupted their song to suggest that they are more alike than they think, they would have been horrified. We have now discovered Mythological Rule #2: *We know we are good because we hate evil.* Each girl knows for sure that she is good because she has proof – her hatred of the one she believes is wicked.

Deriving our sense of ourselves as good in contrast to another is all too common. I have done it many times and I can offer you a particularly painful example. I have a younger sister, we'll call her Betsy, who many years ago asked for my advice with a personal problem. I took a great deal of interest in her, spoke with her often, and even lent her money. In the end, however, she refused the solution I offered her and chose instead to remain in the dead end job she was in, living in the squalid apartment

I was trying to help her leave. I felt as if she had rejected me, not just my advice, and became quite angry with her. I didn't speak to her beyond a perfunctory hello at family events for at least 10 years.

Fortunately we have another sister, we'll call her Ann, who continually tried to reunite us. Finally, at a dinner Ann arranged, I actually listened to Betsy and I realized that she was a very sad and lonely woman who understood her situation better than I did. She hadn't rejected me at all, but was unable to envision a better life for herself, so undeserving of love did she feel. I had been terribly wrong about her and had hurt both of us all those years, but she forgave me without my even asking for forgiveness and we are now the best of friends.

Can you think of a similar situation in your life? Is there someone whom you were convinced was hurtful, mean, and evil in some way, so convinced that you closed yourself off from him only to find out later that you were wrong? If so, you may recognize this part of my confession as your own: I felt really good about myself when I rejected Betsy. I actually puffed up with righteousness, certain that I was right and she had been wrong. I actually used my rejection of Betsy to build up my own self-esteem. It is probably why it took me so long to let go of my anger – it felt too good to give up.

This is an important dynamic to recognize, and one I will return to again and again in the course of this book. Sometimes identifying evil is not really about identifying evil – it is about feeling good about ourselves. When this is the case, it really doesn't matter if what we have found is truly evil or not. It only matters that we believe we have located evil somewhere out there, outside of ourselves. And if we believe in it strongly enough, our sense of ourselves as champions of goodness and truth will inflate like a giant hot air balloon.

We can see this principle operating on an international level as well. What we call patriotism is simply that powerful feeling we get from believing that we are citizens of a good, just nation. But what if, like Elphaba, a nation's positive sense of itself is weak? That nation will do exactly as she did – find a scapegoat who will provide the boost of self-esteem that it so desperately needs. A perfect example of this is the effect of the Treaty of Versailles on Germany at the conclusion of World War I.

ENEMY TWINS

If there is something enemies are sure of, it's that they are nothing alike. Our battles against Nazism and Communism, for example, were battles between opposing forces that stood for different values and ways of life. Totalitarianism versus democracy, repression versus freedom – the fight was cast in terms of irreconcilable opposites. Indeed, the conflicts are often summed up simply as battles between the forces of good and evil. Today's "War on Terror" is characterized in the same way. Yet René Girard warns us of the risk of losing all distinctions between good and evil as the battle rages on. The distinction is much easier to see when the battle is not our own.

Think of the civil war in Rwanda where hundreds of thousands of Tutsis were killed in the 1990s. Or the ethic cleansing carried out by Bosnian Serbs against Croats and Bosnian Muslims in the former Yugoslavia. Or the sectarian violence taking place now in Iraq between Sunni and Shiite Muslims. I must admit to having a hard time keeping the warring parties straight. While each side claims to be distinctly different from their enemy, all that an outsider to the conflict can see is the conflict itself. All claims of morality seem to vanish in the flash of gunfire and rivers of blood. Here is how Girard describes what happens:

> "The antagonists caught up in the … crisis invariably believe themselves separated by insurmountable differences. In reality, however, these differences gradually wear away. Everywhere we now encounter the same desire, the same antagonism, the same strategies – the same illusion of rigid differentiation within a pattern of ever-expanding uniformity. As the crisis grows more acute, the community members are transformed into 'twins,' matching images of violence. I would be tempted to say that they are each doubles of the other."*

...continued on next page

...continued from previous page

Girard points out the inevitable blurring of differences that takes place when hatred consumes both sides, and they each resort to the tactics of violence to achieve their ends. When a Hutu kills a Tutsi or the other way around, neither has a legitimate moral claim, though both would make one. The overwhelming reality is that something terribly evil has happened – a human being has been murdered, and this murder was justified as a good and moral action. I hesitate to offer too many examples like this, because of our tendency to think that we are nothing like the combatants in these examples. We naturally imagine that they are somehow different by virtue of their ethnicity or culture, values or upbringing. The truth is, however, that the only difference between us and the Sunnis and Shiites, for example, is that we do not share their fear and historic antagonism for one another. We have our own fears and historic antagonisms, ones they could not conceive or understand. As any battle escalates, the sense of difference between oneself and one's enemy heightens, even as our mutual violence blurs these differences beyond recognition.

* René Girard. Translated by Patrick Gregory, *Violence and the Sacred*. (Johns Hopkins University Press, 1977) 78-79.

In an effort to punish Germany and secure a lasting peace for Europe, the world humiliated the German nation. Rather than create peace, many commentators at the time "foresaw the seeds of another war sown in the harsh terms imposed by the peacemakers at Versailles."[1] Here is what Hitler wrote about the treaty in Mein Kampf:

> When, in the year 1919, the peace treaty was imposed on the German people, one would have been justified in hoping that the cry for German freedom would be powerfully promoted through this very instrument ... How could this instrument of boundless

> extortion and shameful abasement have become, in the hands of a willing government, a means of whipping up national passions to the boiling point! How, by means of genial propagandistic utilization of these sadistic atrocities, could a people's indifference be raised to indignation, and indignation to the most blazing anger!
>
> How every one of these points could have been burned into the brain and feeling of this nation until, finally, in the heads of sixty million men and women the same sense of shame and the same hate would have become a single fiery sea of flames, out of whose glow a steely will would have risen and a cry forced itself: We want arms once more![2]

Adolf Hitler effectively used the demoralizing elements of the treaty as justification during his rise to power. While there is no excuse for Hitler's crimes against humanity, there is also nothing unique about the mechanism he used to gain power. Anyone or group of people, from cliques to nation states, becomes extremely vulnerable to scapegoating when they feel humiliated and unloved.

Because of her need for approval, Elphaba is particularly susceptible to this false way of feeling good about herself. Elphaba responds to Galinda's blondness and popularity – the very things Elphaba may secretly desire for herself – with instant disdain. We are left to wonder if Elphaba will ever be able to turn the tables on her own trait – will she ever be able to see her greenness as good?

What has happened to these two girls? They began the show as total opposites, one blonde, sparkly and popular, the other green, dark and outcast. One was good, the other evil. But now that they are both consumed with the same emotion – loathing – it has erased all differences between them. It is what we saw happen to Dorothy and the Witch in Baum's book when each was wearing one of the silver shoes. Both the good little girl and the big bad Witch were consumed by their desire to possess the silver shoes and threw identical temper tantrums. The good girl and the bad Witch would stop at nothing, not even murder, to obtain the object of their desire. They became twins, sad doubles of greed and hatred. The same fate has now overtaken Galinda and Elphaba.

has turned Mythological Rule #2 upside down. The ... if you hate what is evil, you are good. The truth is that if you hate what you think is evil, you will become identical to it because hatred turns you into the twin of your enemy. Who is good and who is evil if they are both filled with hatred? Can we say that Galinda's hatred is justified because Elphaba is evil? What if Elphaba is not the evil Witch of the opening celebration, but simply a lonely, misunderstood girl desperate for her father's love and the world's acceptance? Neither girl's hatred of the other can be excused and the question of how to tell good from evil continues to be mired in confusion.

5

Something Bad

The Animals are recalled to the lands of their ancestors, a ploy to give the farmers a sense of control over *something* anyway. It's a systematic marginalizing of populations, Glinda, that's what the Wizard's all about.

MAGUIRE, *Wicked*

The true "scapegoats" are those whom men have never recognized as such, in whose guilt they have an unshaken belief.

RENÉ GIRARD,
Things Hidden Since The Foundation Of The World

By a scapegoat effect I mean that strange process through which two or more people are reconciled for whatever ails, disturbs, or frightens the scapegoaters. They feel relived of their tensions and they coalesce into a more harmonious group. They now have a single purpose, which is to prevent the scapegoat from harming them, by expelling and destroying him.

JAMES G. WILLIAMS, Editor,
The Girard Reader

We are barely fifteen minutes into the musical and *Wicked* has shattered our deeply held assumptions about good and evil, completely upsetting what we thought we knew to be true. As audience members, we are as confused as the Ozians, for we have lost our moorings and are no longer able to trust our instincts.

As we have discussed, this entertaining story with its dazzling sets, fast-paced action, and captivating songs is a Myth-buster of the first order. Schwartz and Holzman have begun dismantling the Myth told about good and evil by asking the question, "Are people born Wicked? Or do they have Wickedness thrust upon them?" In no uncertain terms they answer: People have wickedness thrust upon them completely arbitrarily. Within the Myth, good and evil are shown to be matters of opinion rather than inherent qualities. Like being popular or an outcast, they are changeable things, not fixed traits. The main difference between Galinda and Elphaba is not that one is good and one is evil – it is that Galinda is far better at manipulating the opinion of others than is Elphaba. Galinda's ability to deflect bad impressions and cultivate good ones is the key to her success. And poor Elphaba is not an inherently bad person – she simply stinks at PR.

Is *Wicked* asking us to believe that there are no such things as good or evil? Are we to believe that everything is relative, that we can never know what goodness is or where evil is to be found? According to the musical, we are to believe no such thing. But the Myth threatens us that without its version of the truth our ability to tell good from evil will evaporate. "If you abandon me," the Myth says, "you will be left with a world of chaos and confusion. Is this what you want?" The Myth wants us to believe that it holds a monopoly on identifying good and evil. But that is a lie. Only if we are brave enough to abandon the Myth, will we discover the truth about good and evil. In the next scene, we learn that part of what the Myth does is deliberately blind us so that what is truly evil remains hidden from view. We are offered a way to have our blindness cured and our sight restored through the introduction of an unlikely prophetic voice.

Dr. Dillamond is a Goat. A Goat with a capital G who can talk, think and philosophize like Aristotle. He calls himself the "token Goat" on the faculty of Shiz, a reference to his minority status. In Oz, there is a

WHO NEEDS A CRYSTAL BALL? NOT PROPHETS!

Often prophets are thought of as visionaries with a special power to foretell the future. While there is an element of fortune-telling involved, prophetic insights come not from some mystical power, but from a keen ability to see those things that are hidden from others. Prophets see clearly what we are blind to, not only the truths of our present behavior, but also the future consequences of the path we are on.

Professor Marvel is an example of this in the 1939 movie. By studying Dorothy's clothes, mannerisms and the contents of her basket (a picture of Auntie Em at the farm house gate), he makes a pretty good guess about the future: Auntie Em will be heartsick when she realizes Dorothy has run away, and Dorothy will be so sorry at the suffering she caused her Aunt that she will run home full of remorse. The only gift Professor Marvel had was being a keen observer of people.

Prophets are keen and compassionate observers of societies, extraordinarily sensitive to all human suffering. While you or I can read about an injustice or human tragedy and then forget it when we close the paper, a prophet is affected so profoundly that they cry out in sympathetic pain and feel called to protect the weak and powerless. The prophets of the Hebrew Scriptures give us ample evidence of this as they throw all caution to the wind, forcefully critiquing the kings and power-brokers of their day, insisting that they care for the poor, the widows and orphans. In so doing they risked ostracism, persecution, imprisonment and death.

As Abraham J. Heschel writes in the introduction to his wonderful book *The Prophets*, "The [biblical] prophet was an individual who said 'No' to his society, condemning its habits and assumptions, its complacency and waywardness."* Heschel continues, "The prophet is a lonely man. He alienates the wicked as well as the pious, the cynics as well as the believers, the priests and the princes, the judges and the false prophets."**

Whenever you feel annoyed, irritated or downright angered by someone you feel is criticizing you unjustly, it is entirely possible that you are in the presence of a modern day prophet. A rather uncomfortable thought, isn't it?

* Abraham J. Heschel, *The Prophets*. (New York, NY: Harper & Row, 1962) xxix.
** Ibid, 22.

whole category of animals that can talk and think like humans. They are called Animals, with a capital A to distinguish them from the normal, Kansas-variety animals we are familiar with in our world. It is more than coincidence that Dillamond is a goat and not some other animal. Schwartz and Holzman (like Gregory Maguire in his novel) are fairly hitting us over the head with their obvious reference to a scapegoat. As if the image of a talking goat in academic garb is not striking enough, Schwartz and Holzman treat us to this dialogue:

> DILLAMOND:
> Doubtless you've noticed I am the sole Animal on the faculty – the "token Goat," as it were. But it wasn't always this way. Oh, dear students ... how do I put this? How I wish you could have known this place as it once was. When one would walk down these halls and hear an Antelope explicating a sonnet, a Snow Leopard solving an equation, a Wildebeest waxing philosophic. Can you see, students, what's being lost? How our dear Oz is becoming less and less, well ... (looks right at Elphaba) ... colorful. (Taking in the rest of the class.) Now. What sent this into motion?
>
> ELPHABA:
> (Raises hand.) From what I've heard, it began with the Great Drought.
>
> DILLAMOND:
> Exactly. Precisely. Food grew scarce and people grew hungrier and angrier. And the question became – whom can we blame? Can anyone tell me what is meant by the term: "Scapegoat"?

Before Dr. Dillamond can lead the class in a discussion about scapegoats, he is interrupted by the discovery of a message on the blackboard. It reads: "ANIMALS SHOULD BE SEEN AND NOT HEARD." In dismay and frustration, he dismisses the class. Only Elphaba remains.

This scene brings together many of the elements we have discussed thus far in the book. When the Animals are blamed for the drought,

Rule #1 is in full play. They are being identified as evil and no one is questioning it. Their story is being hidden as the world becomes "less and less... colorful." But not all voices have been silenced. Dr. Dillamond can still speak and remains capable of telling the Animal's perspective. From what we have learned from Girard, we know that this scene is not Mythological because the voice of the victim is present. Rather than a Myth, a victorious telling of the triumph of good over evil, it is what Girard calls a Text of Persecution, an account in which the victim's suffering and unjustified abuse is no longer hidden. The individual who wrote that ominous phrase on the blackboard represents all those who believe in the Mythological version of the history of the drought, and those who have benefited from it as well. They have a vested interest in making sure that history is not rewritten to include the Animals' perspective, as this would upset the balance of power they enjoy.

What is there to gain by concealing the Animals' story? Dr. Dillamond has asked the class about the word "scapegoat." We know what a scapegoat is and how it functions. We don't need a talking goat to tell us that a community can be united, all internal problems resolved (or at least temporarily overlooked), when the entire group focuses its hatred and aggression on destroying a common enemy. We know that Myth depends on just how well the scapegoating process works to win our faithfulness and keep us from asking too many questions.

It seems natural that when people are in crisis there is an instinct to blame someone. Even in a natural disaster like a drought that no human being could have caused, the search for someone to blame begins to consume the community. Why? Because hardships cause discord and dissention as members of the community fight with each other over scarce resources. Imagine what it would be like if there was not enough water for your family. What if you had to compete with your friends and neighbors for water for your child, spouse or sick parent? Terrible tensions and anxiety would begin to build and we can imagine the accusations that would fly through the community – Jim is taking more than his share; Betty is hoarding water in her basement and pretending she has none; Larry deliberately tripped Louise, causing her to spill her ration because she wouldn't go with him to the prom.

THE SCAPEGOAT RITUAL

The modern understanding of a scapegoat has its origins in an ancient ritual described in chapter 16 of the Book of Leviticus. God instructs Moses how his brother Aaron, the high priest, is to conduct a ritual of atonement for the people. Two goats are to be chosen by lot, one to be sacrificed to the Lord and one for "Azazel" which is traditionally translated as "scapegoat." (Girard explains that Azazel is generally thought to be "the name of an ancient demon said to inhabit the desert.")* After the Lord's goat is sacrificed, God tells Moses what to do with the remaining goat:

> [Aaron] shall present the live goat. Then Aaron shall lay both his hands on the head of the live goat, and confess over it all the iniquities of the people of Israel, and all their transgressions, all their sins, putting them on the head of the goat, and sending it away into the wilderness by means of someone designated for the task. The goat shall bear on itself all the iniquities to a barren region; and the goat shall be set free in the wilderness. (Leviticus 16:20-22)

This text reveals more than how to conduct a religious ritual. It exposes the way in which societies operate to cleanse themselves of the destructive forces of envy, hatred, and resentments by selecting and blaming innocent victims. By stating that "the ritual scapegoat is chosen by lot," the text reveals the arbitrary way all scapegoats are chosen. By emphasizing that Aaron places the sins of the people on the head of the live animal, the text shows that all scapegoats are forced to bear the burden of the sins of others. And by banishing the ritual goat, the text demonstrates how we expel our scapegoats from our community rather than face the consequences of our own failings. We'd rather our sins be exiled in the wilderness than come back to rest on our own heads, where they belong.

* *Things Hidden*, 131

Eventually these suspicions and resentments would threaten to destroy the community from within. It is possible that it would not be the drought itself that destroys the community, but the resulting fears and resentments turned violent.

A central thesis of René Girard's theory is that the greatest threat to the existence and well being of human communities is the risk of its own violence turned inward. The scapegoat's function is to "keep the violence *outside* the community."[1] Here Girard describes what can happen when a community suffers a build up of resentment and aggression:

> When relationships between men are troubled, when men cease to cooperate among themselves and to come to terms with one another, there is no human enterprise that does not suffer. Even the success of the hunt, of fishing expeditions, of food gathering is put in question.[2]

Scapegoating someone is an easy way to turn all this internal antagonism onto something outside the community, thus creating unity where once there was conflict. Where once Jim, Betty, Larry and Louise were all fighting amongst themselves, the scapegoat cleanses them of their resentments toward each other. In this case, the scapegoat may actually become the community's salvation – if they believe wholeheartedly in his guilt and wickedness, they can begin working together to solve their problems. Silencing the victim's story is the key to the effectiveness of the scapegoating mechanism.

Even more at stake than the benefits of peace the community experienced by scapegoating the Animals, is the community's sense of themselves as good people. As the crude chalkboard statement attested, Animals should never be heard because to actually hear their cries of pain and anguish, to be confronted with their suffering, would shatter the benefits of Rule #2. How can you know you are good if you are forced to see that the ones you believed were monstrously evil and deserving of death are as "human" as you are? No, the victim's story must never be told. Ever.

Dr. Dillamond sings to Elphaba a catalogue of frightening things rumored to have silenced all the scapegoated Animals:

DILLAMOND:
I've heard of an ox
A professor from Quox
No longer permitted to teach
Who has lost all powers of speech
And an owl in Munchkin Rock
A vicar with a thriving flock
Forbidden to preach
Now he only can screech
Only rumors – but still –
Enough to give pause
To anyone with paws
Something bad is happening in Oz ...

ELPHABA:
Something bad? Happening in Oz ...?

DILLAMOND:
Under the surface
Behind the scenes
Something BAAAAAAD ...
Sorry ... "Bad" ...

Even as Dr. Dillamond sings, he begins to lose his own power of speech, bleating instead of speaking as he says "bad." Elphaba can't believe that something bad could happen in Oz. After all, she believes the Wizard is watching out for the good of all, taking care of everyone from his central point in the Emerald City. Elphaba tells Dr. Dillamond that she is going to the Emerald City herself. After all, she naively tells him, "If something bad is happening to the Animals, someone's got to tell the Wizard! He'll make it right. That's why we *have* a Wizard!"

The Wizard represents the Myth, the High Priest of Peace, the very thing promised to those who believe unquestioningly in whatever story he puts forth. But now we know, at least in part, what the cost is of the peace enjoyed by the Emerald City – the Animals. The peace of Oz is being purchased with their lives. They are being silenced, stripped of their power of speech, which is the essence of their Animalness. If they were humans, we would say they were being robbed of their humanity. Schwartz and Holzman darkly suggest that the Animals are being murdered, the victims of a systematic extermination. Again, if they were human beings, we would be talking about genocide.

Although Dr. Dillamond is still able to tell his story, no one but Elphaba is listening. Only Elphaba stayed behind to hear it and even she, a scapegoating victim herself, is finding it all hard to believe. How is it possible that such an evil thing could be happening in Oz? Oz, the land of Mythological Peace, promises that the truly good have the right and responsibility to destroy the truly evil. Furthermore, Oz assures its citizens that mistakes are never made in this destruction process, especially not on the epic scale of genocide. The good people of Oz and their wonderful leader could certainly not let such a terrible thing happen. But as Elphaba will discover before the end of the first act, such tragic mistakes are inevitable within the Myth. They are the direct outcome of Mythological Rule #3: *There are two kinds of violence – Good Violence and Bad Violence.* It is this belief in Good Violence that permits the good people of Oz to allow such bad things to happen without shaking their faith in themselves as good people. Let's see how it works.

First we need to ask – what is violence? It doesn't seem like a very difficult question to answer. Webster defines violence as "physical force used so as to injure" – punching, biting, kicking, shooting, knifing – anything that causes physical harm falls into this category. I expand Webster's definition a bit because I believe that people can be harmed psychologically, emotionally and spiritually, as well as physically. A child who is verbally or sexually abused, a friend whose trust is betrayed, a person who is excluded from community – all these people are victims of a type of violence as well. Whether my expansion of the definition is commonly accepted or not, in all these examples one thing is clear – the kind of harm we are talking about is a bad thing. No one wants to be a victim of violence, whether physical, psychological or emotional. No one wants to be hurt, slandered, cast out or killed, and anyone who does these things to another human being is at the very least, behaving badly. At worst, they are engaging in evil.

Except under certain conditions. We see them in all Mythological tales, such as the classic good guy/ bad guy stories we live with today. They present a hero who, in his battle against the forces of evil, uses Good Violence to save the world from destruction. These good guys have no qualms about using guns, bombs, lasers, knives and flame-throwers to defeat the enemy. In fact, they are most creative in thinking up ways to kill their adversaries. As an audience, we often thrill and cheer the loudest when the hero kills in a spectacular fashion. Good guys, it seems, have permission to use violence and indeed, are encouraged to do so.

Why don't we accuse good guys of being evil? Isn't violence a bad thing? Doesn't it cause suffering and harm to human beings? Nevertheless, we cheer each and every bad guy that is killed, while we mourn the death of any good guy that the plot allows on the way to ultimate good guy victory. I remember the opening sequence of the movie *True Lies*[3] in which Arnold Schwarzenegger's character runs through the woods shooting at men right and left, while his friend waits to drive him away, joking and teasing about the entire event.

We cheer, of course, because we believe the violence is necessary to protect innocent people from being victims of violence at the hands of the evil enemy. Violence wielded by the good guys is used to prevent the violence of the bad guys and we believe it is perfectly justified. Unfortunately, we now know that the easy categories of good and evil are arbitrary and often false.

It is at the point when the destruction of a bad guy is equated with the peace and salvation of the community, that the Myth's most evil turn occurs. Violence has been compartmentalized and sanitized. No longer a dreaded cause of pain and suffering, violence has become an instrument of peace, the weapon of choice in the battle against evil. This is how we get Mythological Rule #3 and the most devastating consequence of belief in the Myth. The Myth has generated two things where once there was only one. Instead of what we knew as only Violence, the Myth has produced Good Violence and Bad Violence.

Within the Myth, Good Violence occurs when good people kill bad people. Bad Violence happens when bad people kill good people. Similar to our experience with the qualities of good and evil, the Myth has cast a spell over us, confusing and blinding us so that we can commit the most evil deeds while believing ourselves to be morally right. Girard has pointed out that we never think of our own violence as "aggression." The violence we commit is always retaliatory, always provoked and justified. Only the violence used by our enemies is understood as aggressive, unprovoked, and unnecessary.[4]

It is this ability to rationalize our own violence and commit evil without any moral misgivings that is the cost to communities that live by the rules of the Myth. This is hidden in the fine print, the portion of the Myth we must be brave enough to read in full.

Remember how hatred erased all differences between the wicked Elphaba and the good Galinda? Violence does the same thing. When the good and the wicked are both using violence, all differences between them are erased. This equality, however, is not something the perpetrators can see. It is only visible to the victims. The perpetrators – the heroes and villains – believe in the differences between them provided by their ideologies. A hero believes he is acting to save the world, and that a villain acts to further his own interests. Girard puts it this way: "Scapegoating has never been conceived by anyone as an activity in which he himself participates and may still be participating even as he denounces the scapegoating of others."[5]

But protestations and claims of morality made by perpetrators of violence matter little to the bystander who is injured or killed. Dead is dead and the explanation can't bring back the life of a loved one. Whether someone dies as a victim of a terrorist attack or as collateral damage in a US bombing raid, the grief felt by their family is the same. Just as Elphaba and Galinda insisted that they were nothing at all alike, so do the antagonists involved in any conflict. When both sides use violence, no assertion of difference, no matter how eloquent or insistent, can conceal forever how they have become twins of one another, enemy twins locked in combative violence that can end only with the total surrender or complete annihilation of the other.

What is interesting for those trying to break free of the Myth is how the hero and the villain function as scapegoats for one another. Each perceives the other as evil, as the sole obstacle to achieving their aims, and whose very existence is untenable. Both the hero and villain believe that the destruction of the other is the only way for their own life to continue. Now, here is the distinction that the Myth does not want us to make: Finding and using a scapegoat can make you feel good about yourself and bring peace to your community. But it is a false peace that is purchased at the expense of innocent victims. Peace and true goodness are possible, but never when the suffering of innocent people is a necessary condition.

Of course, the tricky part is, how can we make an accurate determination about who is innocent and who is evil? One thing that is sure to help is an understanding of how scapegoated victims are chosen within the Myth. The more we understand that process, the better we will be at spotting it when it happens. Oz, during the drought, is an ideal example because the scapegoating of the Animals exposes the arbitrary nature of the whole process. We also saw this occur with Elphaba's green skin – there was nothing inherently evil about it, it just happened to be an obvious outward sign that marked her as different and thus a target to be scapegoated.

Animals are a small minority within Oz, a unique and easily identifiable group so they are at risk within the Myth from the outset. This is obvious to us in our own world where minority groups require special protection under the law to prevent them from being victims of persecution from the broader community. Two obvious barriers to opportunity have always been gender and race – neither of which can be chosen or changed. Religious affiliation and sexual orientation have also been especially prone to persecution because members of these groups can be so easily labeled.

But there is another factor besides just unique outward signs – the scapegoat must not pose a threat of retaliatory violence. In other words, if the Animals had a way to protect themselves – a weapon or champion to defend them – persecuting them would pose a threat to the peace of the community. Persecution or annihilation wouldn't ensure peace but might enflame a larger conflict. For example, Nessarose is not a scapegoat because in spite of the differentiating mark of her disability, she has a champion in

REFUGEE OR TERRORIST?

On the surface, it seems like a reasonable idea: prevent anyone belonging to or supporting rebel groups from entering our country. Identify those willing to use violence, and don't let them inside our borders. This is, in fact, a provision of the USA Patriot Act and the Real ID Act, and it appears to be a sensible measure taken to keep terrorists out of America. But there's a problem: By preventing all people who use or support the use of violence from entering our country, we are keeping out some of our friends. Thousands fleeing the authoritarian government of Myanmar, hundreds of refugees from Vietnam and Laos who fought alongside US forces during the Vietnam war, and dozens of Cubans who supported armed resistance against Castro have been denied resettlement in the United States by the State Department.*

The instinct of these laws is good – that all violence is bad – but the Myth insists that not all violence is bad all the time. Only the violence used by our enemies is bad. Our violence, as well as the violence of those who support our beliefs and political agendas, is not bad at all and should not be punished. So we are left with a rather confusing legal situation. It becomes impossible to distinguish between the "terrorists" and the "refugees" solely on the basis of their willingness to use violence. We need to provide a further clarification: Those willing to use violence against our enemies are our friends and deserve refugee status; those willing to use violence against our friends or us are our enemies and therefore terrorists. The violence of our enemies is perceived as destructive and unable to yield anything positive, while our violence is a force for peace and good.

Congress and the State Department are working now to adjust the laws to favor our friends, providing an excellent example of the distinction we unquestioningly make between Good and Bad Violence and the difficulty of doing so with moral integrity.

*Rachel L. Swarns, "Terror Laws Cut Resettlement of Refugees," New York Times, 28 Sept. 2006: A21.

her father, the Governor of Munchkinland. If Nessarose were a victim of violence, the Governor would avenge himself on the perpetrator thereby defending the victim and escalating the violence rather than bringing peace. And if Nessarose's victimizer were another powerful person, let us say the Wizard himself, then all out war might erupt in Oz. Those who use violence to maintain peace must be very careful under what conditions they employ it. As easily as violence can bring peace it can also lead to an increase in violence and the ultimate destruction of the community.

An interesting example of this on an international level is the cold war that existed between the US and the USSR from the 1950's until 1989. Countries allied themselves with one power or the other as a defensive maneuver, knowing that if they had a champion, they could enjoy a measure of protection from attack themselves. Neither power wanted to risk escalation to an active war, so the threat of retaliatory violence kept each country in check. The threat of all-out international warfare during all those years kept the world holding its breath – the smallest retaliatory conflict risked unleashing nuclear weapons and the potential for tremendous global destruction. This ultimate threat of violence prevented the two powers from using their own violent weapons against one another for many years.

In order for the Myth to prevail, a scapegoated victim must be someone who is powerless and without allies so that the Good Violence can bring peace and not the threat of more violence. They must be people without a voice, whose story can be easily silenced. Usually they are an already marginalized group of people who have limited power within the society. Jews in the Third Reich, African-Americans in the aftermath of the Civil War, immigrants and the poor across cultures and nations are all classic victims because they bear easily distinguishing marks and their annihilation poses no risk to the community.

As the feuding Hatfields and McCoy's taught us, it is possible that someone who is truly guilty of something can still be an innocent victim. Another example of this strange paradox is the classic good guy/bad guy movie, the American Western. A popular plot goes something like this: The good guy is the sheriff and the bad guy is a murderer or cattle rustler or both. The bad guy is in jail waiting for the circuit judge to come, but rather than wait for the judge the good people of the town form a lynch mob to handle the situation themselves. After all, the bad guy's guilt is not in doubt. But the sheriff insists on protecting the bad guy murderer against the good guys and wait for the judge to arrive. The sheriff tells the good people of the town that they are behaving badly and that vigilante justice does not justify committing murder.

How could that be true? How could the good people of the town be wrong for killing a murderer? For two reasons: (1) If the lynch mob is using the death of the bad guy in the same way that the Ozians used Elphaba's death – to know they are good by identifying and destroying evil – then there is something morally ambiguous about the situation. And (2) the judicial system alone is empowered to wield Good Violence. The very same violence – the hanging of the cattle rustler – is good when used by the state but bad when used by a lynch mob. The legal and judicial system is actually an attempt to narrowly define the circumstances in which violence is good and to claim the use of Good Violence for the state. While still operating within the Myth, it is an attempt to introduce morality into a system that inherently lacks it.

So let's summarize what we know about the use of Good Violence against a scapegoat. A scapegoat is someone who is innocent of their accused crimes, but who is nevertheless found to be guilty by the community, like the Animals during the drought. The scapegoat's function is to cleanse the society of its internal conflicts and bring peace to the community. In other words, the scapegoat is being charged with the failings, aggression and anger of the community. Whether the scapegoat is technically innocent, like the Animals or the Jews in Germany, or technically guilty like a chicken thief or cattle rustler, doesn't matter in the least. The innocence or guilt of the scapegoat has no relevance; rather it is made to bear responsibility for the crimes of the community. Girard and the scholars who study and interpret his work call this concept "structural innocence."

So a scapegoat can either be guilty of the charge of evil or be completely innocent, so long as they are powerless and everyone within the community agrees that the charge of evil is true. There must be breast-beating, mob-thrilling unanimity in the accusation. If there is any doubt about the exercise of Good Violence, as the doubt that creeps into the Ozian mob when Galinda suggests a friendship with the Witch, the effectiveness of the scapegoating process will be undermined. After all, the point of the whole exercise is to locate evil somewhere outside of the community and then expel it from our midst. It all depends on our certainty that we have indeed located the evil. Any doubt at all and the whole thing falls apart. We can see that with Elphaba – she has high regard for Dr. Dillamond and is not convinced at all by the accusations against the Animals. So Dr. Dillamond does not become a scapegoat for Elphaba.

Elphaba and Dr. Dillamond sing the scene sadly to a close. Elphaba's disbelief that the Animals are being silenced and possibly killed is the very thing upon which the Myth depends. As long as no one suspects that an innocent person is being blamed for their own ills, then no one will challenge the workings of the Myth. The belief in Good Violence will be intact.

ELPHABA:
So nothing bad ...

DILLAMOND:
I hope you're right.

BOTH:
Nothing all that bad

DILLAMOND:
Nothing truly BAAAAAAD ...
Sorry—Bad ...

ELPHABA:
It couldn't happen here
In Oz ...

6

The Unexamined Life

The result justifies the deed. (Exitus acta probat)

OVID, *Heorides* (c. 10 BC)

The first sign of corruption in a society that is still alive is that the end justifies the means.

GEORGES BERNANOS,
Last Essays (1888 – 1948)

The unexamined life is not worth living.

SOCRATES

Passion makes the world go round. Love just makes it a safer place.

ICE T, *The Ice Opinion*

This story of the not-so-wicked witch is not like any fairy tale or Myth we have heard before. At this point in the musical, Schwartz and Holzman have opened our eyes to the lies behind the usual methods of telling the good witch from the bad witch. We can no longer believe that green skin and black clothes designate evil or that blonde hair and white clothes designate good. The "evil" Elphaba, whose death has caused rejoicing throughout the land, is not evil at all, but rather is a lonely girl who has been rejected by her father and is filled with compassion for Dr. Dillamond and the Animals. And Galinda, the paragon of goodness, is merely a popular yet superficial girl who judges others as she judges herself – by outward appearances.

But as we have noted, it is not the existence of good and evil that is being called into question, but the typical methods we use to identify them. Who is the "we" I am referring to here? The Land of Oz is not an allegorical representation of another nation, such as the United States, but it is a metaphor for all human communities, of any size or political leaning.

We all know how successful the scapegoat mechanism is at bringing harmony to a community. From water cooler gossip to political arguments to petty feuds, sacrificing one person or group of people for the greater good is extraordinarily effective. It is a principle that many accept without questioning and has been a vital part of human culture for thousands of years. In fact, Girard would assert that it is the founding mechanism of human culture.

The dynamics of the scapegoat mechanism can be phrased another way as well: the ends justify the means. In other words, if the end goal is a peaceful community, then it is okay to sacrifice one person or a designated group of people so the peace can be preserved. The Myth told about good and evil gives rise to a whole network of relationships that operate on the principle that it is better for a few to suffer so that the many can be saved. This introduces Mythological Rule #4, called *The Sacrificial Formula: Someone can be sacrificed for my good or the good of my community. The End justifies the Means.* Scapegoating is its logical outcome. The code of conduct that depends on the Sacrificial Formula and believes that the end justifies the means is called the Sacrificial System.

THE FIRST CITY

In Genesis, the first book of the Bible, we find an interesting story about the origin of the first city. You may remember Cain, the man who killed his brother Abel in a fit of jealousy because he believed that God favored Abel's meat offering over Cain's offering of grain. After this murder, Genesis 4:17 says: "Cain knew his wife, and she conceived and bore Enoch; and he built a city, and named it Enoch after his son Enoch." Before this, no city had been mentioned in all of creation. Girard interprets this to mean that the first city was made possible by the peace purchased by a scapegoating murder.

The story of Cain and Abel sounds similar to the story of two other brothers, gods who founded the city of Rome. Romulus kills his brother Remus in another fit of sibling rivalry and Rome is born from divine anger. But Girard insists that while the story of the founding of Rome is indeed a Myth, the Genesis tale is not. Why? Because in the Genesis story, the victim's voice is not silenced.

In response to God's probing question, "Where is your brother Abel?" Cain evades responsibility with the rather flip remark, "Am I my brother's keeper?" When God says in 4:10, "What have you done? Listen; your brother's blood is crying out to me from the ground!" we are told that God himself hears the victim's voice and suffers with him. In the Myth about Rome, the god Romulus never weeps for his brother. Remus is never heard from again, and the victim's voice is effectively silenced by his death. While both narratives explain the founding of cities, the Roman Myth never questions the divine justice of the murder. It is only within the biblical narrative that we find voices that dare to question the logic that violence is endorsed by the divine to create peace in human communities.

The cost of the peace enjoyed by participants in the Sacrificial System is becoming startlingly clear. Not only are innocent victims sacrificed for our benefit, our own goodness is compromised in the process. Once we recognize the suffering of our victims, our sense of ourselves as morally good people begins to teeter. How can we see ourselves as good, moral beings if that status rests on the victimization of others? There are other costs to us as well, and in the next few scenes the musical attempts to demonstrate the destructive power of Sacrificial Systems on the everyday lives of those who participate in and benefit from it. Let's follow the action.

Enter a new character that epitomizes the virtue most valued by the Myth – blindness. Fiyero arrives as the wealthy, aristocratic, handsome new student at Shiz University who completely dazzles Galinda with his prestige. He is a Winkie Prince and his very presence sends her little, superficial heart aflutter. He is delighted to learn that he has arrived too late for history class and scoffs at Boq's assertion that the main occupation of the students at Shiz is studying. Fiyero sings:

> The trouble with schools is
> They always try to teach the wrong lesson
> Believe me, I've been kicked out
> Of enough of them to know
> They want you to become less callow
> Less shallow
> But I say: Why invite stress in?
> Stop studying strife
> And learn to live "The Unexamined Life" ...

This is a very clever and concise summation of the promises made by the Myth: As long as no one questions the accusations of evil too closely, the community will be safe. Remain callow and shallow, swallowing the Mythic version of good and evil, and your life will be stress free. His song continues, glorifying the virtues of deliberate ignorance.

Dancing through life
Skimming the surface
Gliding where turf is smooth
Life's more painless
For the brainless
Why think so hard?
When it's so soothing
Dancing through life
No need to tough it
When you can sluff it off as I do
Nothing matters
But knowing nothing matters
It's just life
So keep dancing through ...

Not only is being brainless a virtue to Fiyero, but there is no reason to doubt it because he implies that life itself doesn't matter. This is the Myth itself waving its hand in front of our faces to induce cooperation the way Obi Wan Kenobi in the Star Wars saga can wave his hand in front of the weak-minded and secure their obedience to his will. Nothing matters, proclaims the Myth, except your own happiness – certainly not the suffering of one victim. So just keep dancing the scapegoat dance.

Dancing through life
Mindless and careless
Make sure you're where less
Trouble is rife
Woes are fleeting
Blows are glancing
When you're dancing
Through life...

With these lyrics we have the perfect statement of allegiance to the Myth, and they begin with a series of interactions between the main characters that are at best morally ambiguous, and at worst downright manipulative. I believe we can view each of these little plot moves as an illustration of the types of human relationships that are common in communities under the spell of Myth.

GALINDA AND BOQ

The musical offers no explanation as to the reason Boq is infatuated with Galinda. There is an assumption that his infatuation needs no explanation. Galinda's appearance is the epitome of desirability in the Mythic culture: pretty and stylish, a fashion expert. After all, what is fashion, if not the ability to distinguish between which trend is good (as in good taste) and which is bad. The rise and fall of fashion trends is a perfect metaphor for the arbitrary nature of the labels of "good" and "evil." In fact, the tyranny of fashion is a symptom of a culture dependent on Myth. The hemline that represents good taste one season is incredibly tacky the next, yet neither is inherently more "fashionable" than the other. Madison Avenue convinces us, however, that those who traipse around in last year's fashions are ridiculous creatures worthy of ridicule. Do we choose our love objects in the same way, by how well they embody arbitrary and artificial outward signs of desirability and goodness? If so, we are in the same boat as Boq – infatuated with something that doesn't really exist.

BOQ AND NESSAROSE

Boq is in love with Galinda, who is good by all outward appearances. How does Galinda respond to this adoration? She sees Boq as an obstacle to attaining the true object of her desire, Fiyero. Galinda clearly fears that if Boq hangs around her all the time, his average reputation may rub off on her. She thinks she may become less desirable to Fiyero simply by her association with someone of a lower social status. To get rid of Boq, Galinda uses his feelings of infatuation against him. She pretends that her heart's desire is for the wellbeing of Nessarose, the "tragically beautiful girl" in the wheelchair. Galinda suggests to Boq that she might return his love if he can help her make Nessarose happy. So off Boq goes, to pretend to love Nessarose so he can win the object of his desire, Galinda.

The set-up is clear: Galinda manipulates Boq (Means) to win Fiyero's love (her End) and Boq deceives Nessarose (Means) to win Galinda's affection (his End). This is the Sacrificial Formula being extended in small ways through everyday relationships. For if a small dose of suffering inflicted on a scapegoat victim is allowed for the greater good of a community, then a small dose of immoral behavior can easily be allowed to achieve one's own personal desires. It is a cynical and self-centered calculation, but it is a logical outcome of a Sacrificial System.

GALINDA AND FIYERO

Fiyero witnesses how expertly Galinda uses her charms and Boq's infatuation to her advantage and acknowledges with the compliment, "You're good." Remember, Fiyero is representative of the Sacrificial System, so his pronouncement that Galinda is good at her manipulation is an affirmation from the perspective of that system. The willingness to use whatever means possible to rid yourself of obstacles to your desire is highly prized in the Sacrificial System. We all know the saying, "all's fair in love and war," and we can now recognize it as a motto of Myth.

Galinda and Fiyero now sing a duet in which they are mirror images of each other.

GALINDA:
Now that we've met one another,

BOTH:
It's clear – We deserve each other

GALINDA:
You're perfect!

FIYERO:
You're perfect!

BOTH:
So we're perfect together
Born to be forever ...
Dancing through life ...

They are perfect examples of the ruthlessness tolerated and encouraged within the Sacrificial System. But not surprisingly, in a Myth-busting musical like *Wicked*, something happens that shakes Galinda's confidence in the morality of her behavior.

GALINDA AND ELPHABA

To free herself from Boq's unwanted attention, Galinda convinces him to take Nessarose to the party. Nessarose is overwhelmed by Boq's invitation, and although she knows he asked her at Galinda's urging she acts completely unaware of Boq's underlying motivation. Why has she chosen to ignore the truth? It is not made entirely clear, but Nessarose claims she is "about to have the first happy night of [her] life, thanks to Galinda!" Elphaba seems skeptical. It is hard for her to believe that Galinda might act unselfishly.

Indeed, Galinda's heartlessness is being demonstrated out of earshot of Elphaba. She is looking for the appropriate clothing to "accessorize" herself for Fiyero when she uncovers an obviously unfashionable, pointy, black hat her granny had given her. "I'd give it away," she tells her friends, "but I don't hate anyone that much!" But her friends suggest that perhaps there is someone they all hate that much, and they turn their eyes on the fast-approaching Elphaba. Before Elphaba can ask Galinda about her motives in setting up Boq and Nessarose, Galinda offers her the hat as an unexpected gift.

Galinda lies to Elphaba, much to her friends' delight, telling Elphaba that the ugly thing is the height of fashion and that Elphaba should wear it to the party tonight. Scapegoats deserve whatever they get, and it is clear that Galinda and her friends enjoy renewed solidarity over this cruel joke.

Elphaba has nothing to say to Galinda in the face of this gift. She takes the hat and exits the stage, leaving the audience to wonder what

HIGH SCHOOL CLIQUES

High school is often a difficult and painful time, as teenagers – busy forming their identities and sense of self – experiment with different role models. They actually try on identities through their clothes, hairstyles, choice of activities and friends. As we have seen, one sure fire way to know who you are is to have a scapegoat, someone who you are definitely not. This is the energizing force behind high school cliques. Those young people whose sense of self is weak will gravitate toward someone from whom they can acquire it. The leader of a clique often seems like a King or Queen who can bestow a feeling of worth with a glance. The approval of the clique is everything; to lose it feels akin to losing one's life. That is why so many teens will do dangerous and destructive things in order to maintain their connection to the clique, for it is the source of their very being.

The outcasts who are chosen as scapegoats suffer feelings of inferiority and worthlessness because they believe the lies of the clique, that they are evil and the clique has the monopoly on goodness. Identity formation within the Mythological world is a dangerous and painful undertaking. Like love, it must be acquired from someone else and always has strings attached. Like peace, it carries the hidden price of an innocent victim.

she will do next. But shortly Madame Morrible enters looking for Galinda. Here's what happens:

MORRIBLE:
Oh, Miss Upland?

GALINDA:
Madame Morrible ... What are you doing here?

MORRIBLE:
I have something for you. (She hands her a small wand.)

GALINDA:
Oh, Madame ... A training wand! How can I ever express my graditution?

MORRIBLE:
Don't thank me. This was your roommate's idea, not mine.

GALINDA:
(Completely thrown.) What? Elphaba?

MORRIBLE:
Yes. Miss Elphaba requested that I include you in sorcery class. She insisted I tell you this very night or she would quit the seminar.

GALINDA:
But ... why?

MORRIBLE:
I have no idea. My personal opinion is you do not have what it takes. I hope you'll prove me wrong ... I doubt you will.

Until now, Galinda had been denied entrance into Morrible's sorcery class, the very subject she was most excited to study upon her arrival at

Shiz. Elphaba's admittance to the sorcery class only cemented Galinda's hate for the green-skinned outcast. But Galinda's insincere gift of the hat changes things. Now that Elphaba believes that Galinda is extending a kindness to her, Elphaba returns in kind, securing Galinda a space in the coveted sorcery class, and giving Galinda what she wanted in the first place.

Fiyero approaches Galinda as she stands dumbfounded, staring at the small wand Morrible has given her. "What is it?" he asks.

GALINDA:
I got what I wanted ...

FIYERO:
Then what's the matter?

GALINDA:
Nothing ...

FIYERO:
Good. Let's dance ...

Is this the first time Galinda has been given something she wanted without her having to take it by force or forceful guile? Suddenly, everything she thought she knew about Elphaba – that because Elphaba possessed the things Galinda wanted (the gift of magical powers, admittance into the sorcery class) she was an adversary, an obstacle to destroy – is called into question. How could Elphaba be simply *giving* her the very thing she wanted?

Before Galinda can process all of this, Elphaba enters the ballroom proudly wearing the ugly black hat. The students laugh and stare, making mean comments about the way she is dressed. Fiyero asks, "Who in Oz is this?" and Galinda answers, "My roommate. Please don't stare." But Fiyero can't help it and neither can the others. Galinda's joke has worked perfectly. Elphaba is being totally humiliated because she believed Galinda that the hat was the height of fashion. Galinda is now up, as high as the seesaw can take her, and Elphaba is so low that her one wish must be to completely disappear from view.

Elphaba now understands that the hat was not a gift, but a weapon in this petty war of popularity and control. Too proud to show how hurt she is, Elphaba begins to slowly dance alone, rather horribly and without any music, wearing the object of ridicule defiantly on her head.

FIYERO:
Well I'll say this much for her – she doesn't give a twig about what anyone else thinks.

GALINDA:
Of course she does, she just pretends not to ... Oh, I feel awful ...

FIYERO:
Why? It's not like it's your fault.

Galinda knows it is her fault and rather than pretend, she bravely chooses to face her own complicity in someone else's suffering. She leaves Fiyero and walks over to Elphaba. This courageous move is perhaps the most dramatic moment in the musical. Galinda, who has been careful to manipulate her image so that her status is always protected, stands beside the lowest person on the social totem pole at Shiz. In that moment, she chooses to stand with the victim – a victim of her own making – and risk becoming an object of ridicule herself.

But Galinda's powers are strong. Her social status is so powerfully accepted that rather than bring herself down, she can actually elevate Elphaba's status. Galinda asks Elphaba, "May I cut in?" and begins to dance just as horribly as Elphaba. The students, who a moment ago were ridiculing Elphaba, now begin imitating Elphaba's dance moves as they sing a slightly different refrain:

Dancing through life
Down at the Ozdust
If only because dust
Is what we come to
And the strange thing:

Your life could end up changing
While you're dancing
Through!

In this last scene we have seen how the Sacrificial System corrupts all human relationships through blindness and confusion. Any mistreatment of another human being is justified as long as it is in service of the greater good – our own desires. These cruelties and heartless manipulations fall far short of murder, the ultimate means to the end of peace and harmony, but they are no less deadly as they destroy the human heart and trample the human soul.

As the scene ends with Galinda and Elphaba dancing together in defiance of public opinion, we wonder if perhaps they have formed a new friendship and impacted their community along the way. Galinda's false gesture in giving Elphaba her hat generated an unexpected outcome – kindness. Perhaps even a pretend act of selflessness could spark a new relationship – one based on a reciprocal generosity rather than violent or abusive acts. The gift of the hat is reciprocated with the gift of the wand, and that selfless act prompts the greatest gift of all – the willingness to sacrifice of yourself for a friend. Galinda's willingness to dance with Elphaba protects her from a cruelty that can wound as deeply as any act of physical violence.

Have Schwartz and Holzman proved how harmful living under the spell of the Scapegoat Mechanism is? Have they suggested an alternative way to build lasting, peaceful communities? If at this point in the musical you and I can answer yes to these questions, it is more than Elphaba and Galinda can do. Their friendship is tentative at best and must endure many more trials before their story ends.

7

Popular

My definition of a free society is a society where it is safe to be unpopular.

ADLAI E. STEVENSON JR.

I don't think anyone can DO anything that would make him worthy of love. Love is a gift and cannot be earned. It can only be given.

REAL LIVE PREACHER

Nobody ever suggested a leader isn't just as much a scapegoat as a lowly peon.

MAGUIRE, *Wicked*

A new kind of giving has been introduced into the swirl of desires cycloning among the friends and enemies of the musical. It is the novel, unimaginable concept of unconditional giving that asks nothing in return. Even the simulation of such a self-negating act, such as Galinda's insincere gift of the ugly hat to Elphaba, causes profound changes in relationships. Remember, the relationship between Galinda and Elphaba has been rooted in the understanding and belief of the Sacrificial System. That sort of understanding is almost a creed or religion, if you understand a religion to be a cultural system that defines who the gods are and how they are to be worshiped. The creed of the Sacrificial System is one of self-worship.

CREED OF SELF-WORSHIP

- I believe in one god – myself.
- Fulfillment of my desires is the ultimate good.
- Anyone or anything that gets in the way of the fulfillment of my desires is my enemy and subject to destruction by any means available.

Adherence to the Creed of Self-Worship leads to the interactions we saw in the last scene where people were viewed as objects, and hatred and desire were the connective tissue that held people in a relationship. The characters are:

1. Bound by hatred and locked in an endless cycle of wicked reprisals (Galinda and Elphaba), or
2. They are bound to their fellows through agreement over the hate object, the scapegoat (Galinda and her friends), or
3. They are bound to love objects whose desirability is designated by socially agreed upon standards (Boq loves Galinda, Galinda loves Fiyero) or designated by models with high social standing (Morrible and Elphaba love Nessarose because Frex loves her).

As you can see, this Creed leads to relationships that are either based upon, or inevitably generate, hatred and resentments. The scapegoat becomes an essential feature of such a system with so many people who are being wounded, hurt, and caught up in feuding with no end. Unless these hatreds and resentments are focused outward on a scapegoat, what would be left is a community populated by relationships that looked like Galinda's and Elphaba's when they sang "What Is This Feeling?" All the hatreds would remain within the community, creating discord and disunity, sowing chaos. All distinctions between individuals would disappear as hatred turns everyone into mirror images of each other. Such a community would be incapable of cooperating on the simplest of projects and would inevitably disintegrate under its own destructive force, not unlike the whirling of a cyclone that destroys everything in its path.

Unless they find a scapegoat. As Dr. Dillamond has darkly warned us, the Animals are being destroyed and the reason for such destruction has nothing to do with the Animals themselves. They were the arbitrary victims chosen to absorb the resentments and funnel them outside the community. The Animals are the price to be paid for the peace of Oz.

The last scene ended with a note of hope. We were given a glimpse of relationships rooted in the reciprocity of generosity. Simply put, rather than relationships of hatred we have glimpsed relationships of love. Strangely and unexpectedly, Elphaba and Galinda have overcome their resentments without scapegoating anyone. They have formed a community of two through acts of selfless giving.

Love gives without asking for anything in return. The dark Creed of Self-Worship only gives with the expectation of gain. This is the creed openly stated by the Wizard in L. Frank Baum's original story. When Dorothy asked for the Wizard's help to return to Kansas, he said, "You have no right to expect me to send you back to Kansas unless you do something for me in return. In this country everyone must pay for everything he gets." In fact, that could be the motto of the religion we are describing: "Everyone must pay for everything he gets." No generosity of spirit here. The rules of this kingdom as merciless and cruel: tit-for-tat, an eye for an eye, you scratch my back I'll scratch yours.

– her secret about how to manipulate public opinion in her favor. Her song "Popular," is perhaps the most popular song of the musical. It is a primer on how to follow the rules of the current trends to display your popularity for all to see.

> You're gonna be popular!
> I'll teach you the proper ploys
> When you talk to boys
> Little ways to flirt and flounce
> I'll show you what shoes to wear
> How to fix your hair
> Everything that really counts
>
> To be popular!
> I'll help you be popular!
> You'll hang with the right cohorts
> You'll be good at sports
> Know the slang you've got to know
> So let's start
> 'Cause you've got an awf'lly long way to go...

It's a simple formula anyone can follow, and she shares with Elphaba what comes naturally to her without any expectations of gain or self-promotion. Here she reveals the heart of the Sacrificial Mechanism – that no one is inherently good or evil, it's all about manipulating public opinion.

> When I see depressing creatures
> With unprepossessing features
> I remind them on their own behalf
> To think of
> Celebrated heads of state or
> Specially great communicators
> Did they have brains or knowledge?
> Don't make me laugh!

JUICY SCANDAL

Have you ever wondered why we find it so fascinating to read about the foibles of movie stars? Why are we riveted to Miss America's drug problems, Tom Cruise's antics on Oprah's couch or Mel Gibson's hate-filled racial tirades? Celebrities are people we profess to love and admire, yet we take such unabashed glee in reading about their character flaws and bad behavior. It's because we use our fallen celebrities as scapegoats as surely as the Ozian crowd used Elphaba.

That seems an odd claim: What do the winner of a beauty contest and an awkward green girl have in common? Well, they are both part of an easily identifiable minority group. That does two things for us: We can easily identify who they are (not us!), and we can be sure they will have few family members or friends to rise to their defense because there aren't many of them in the first place.

Scapegoats can wear tiaras and designer gowns as easily as ugly black hats. Those at the pinnacle of success and popularity are often aware that they are at risk of being scapegoated. They realize that they are being carefully watched for the slightest misstep that can be turned quickly into the spectacle we thrive on. There is nothing so satisfying as witnessing the fall of the high and mighty. Such gossip is the tamer cousin of the blood lust of the Ozian mob, yet it achieves the same thing: a sense of unity and purpose at the expense of a victim. With the downfall of celebrities, it is the victim's reputation that is shattered rather than his or her physical life, but the dynamic is the same.

When we find ourselves riveted to celebrity news, it may be that rather than participating in "harmless" entertainment, we are practicing the methods of the Sacrificial System. Because practice makes perfect, scapegoating behavior may come to feel natural to us, even good, making it difficult to detect in our real lives with the real people we know and profess to love and admire.

They were popular! Please –
It's all about popular!
It's not about aptitude
It's the way you're viewed
So it's very shrewd to be
Very very popular
Like me!

It's not about aptitude, it's the way you're viewed. This is news to Elphaba. Though she knows that society's view of Galinda as goodness personified is a lie, she does not realize the same thing about herself. In her heart, she believes what the world and her father think – that there is something inherently wrong about her. Just before the "Popular" song begins, Elphaba reveals a secret to Galinda.

ELPHABA:
My father hates me.

GALINDA:
(Gasps.)

ELPHABA:
No, that's not the secret. It's my fault...

GALINDA:
What... what is?

ELPHABA:
... that my sister is the way she is. (Pause.) You see, when my mother was carrying Nessa, my father began to worry that the new baby might come out –

BOTH:
Green.

ELPHABA:

He was so worried he made my mother chew milk flowers, day and night. Only it made Nessa come too soon ... with her little legs all tangled. And our mother – never woke up. None of which ever would have happened ... if not for me.

GALINDA:

But – that was the milk flowers' fault, not yours! That may be your secret, Elphaba. But that doesn't make it true.

Because Frex blames Elphaba for Nessarose's birth defect and his wife's death, Elphaba blames herself, too. But Galinda won't have any of it. She, of all people, knows that just because people think something doesn't make it true. If Elphaba could understand the workings of the Scapegoat Mechanism, she would see that her true worth has nothing to do with what people think about her. What people think can be manipulated easily with the right clothes and make-up. Elphaba's reputation is just a lie told by society, and her father, so that they can use her as a scapegoat with a clear conscience.

At this point, Galinda can carry her experiment in giving only so far. This is her first attempt at genuine friendship, and it is quite an extraordinary one. But it has its limits. The ultimate test of love is whether one is willing to give everything one has, even one's life, for another. We will see such a love in Act II. But for now, we have Galinda's tentative first step out of the sacrificial world and into a new way of being. Galinda will help Elphaba so long as Elphaba does not present a threat to her position in the social structure. She will help Elphaba become popular, but she sings, "Just not quite as popular as me!"

8

The Silence of Progress

Bad temper is its own scourge. Few things are more bitter than to feel bitter. A man's venom poisons himself more than his victim.

CHARLES BUXTON

Men are not the enemy, but the fellow victims. The real enemy is women's denigration of themselves.

BETTY FRIEDAN,
US feminist (1921 – 2006)

When I discover who I am, I'll be free.

RALPH ELLISON

The Sacrificial System is part of the air breathed by the inhabitants of Oz, informing how they understand themselves and their world. It is a pervasive and invisible part of their lives, like the strings on a puppet. They believe with all their hearts that they are independent and autonomous beings, but the inhabitants of the Mythological world are blind to the Myth, blind to the suffering of their victims, and blind to their own culpability. They believe with all their hearts that they are good people and could never suspect otherwise.

Well, not *never*. Not everyone is completely under the spell of the Myth. In the next scene we meet characters that are extracting themselves from the Mythological world. Waking up and opening one's eyes to the truth about the Sacrificial System is an often painful and slow process.

As we follow the action of the musical, we will examine each character to determine how far they have extricated themselves from the Myth or even if they have begun at all. Elphaba exposes the most dangerous and difficult pitfalls of such a journey, making her the undeniable heroine of the story. Let's pick up the action where we left off.

The scene opens in Dr. Dillamond's classroom when Elphaba arrives fresh from Galinda's popularity makeover session. Her frock is improved slightly and her hair is down. She is even practicing the "toss, toss" flip of her hair that Galinda assured her was the way to attract boys. Here Elphaba is displaying the behavior of a person still under the spell of the Myth – she has learned some new rules of how to be successful within the Mythological world and she is trying to follow them to the letter. She doesn't question; she just obeys. She meets Fiyero, however, who suddenly seems far more perceptive than Elphaba.

He comments that she has been "Galinda-fied" and tells her, "You don't need to do that, you know." Elphaba didn't know that, and neither did Fiyero until the moment he saw her mimicking Galinda so obediently. Suddenly his eyes are opened to his poor judgment about both women. His focus was entirely on their outward appearances, and he realizes that appearances are changeable, unreliable and no real indication of what is inside. Suddenly, Elphaba can no longer function as a scapegoat for Fiyero, and the bond he had with Galinda frays. The sense of superiority that Fiyero and Galinda shared over Elphaba and other similarly uncool, unsophisticated classmates has vanished. Perhaps he has been influenced by Galinda's newfound friendship with Elphaba, but whatever the reason, his disdain of Elphaba has disappeared. Fiyero, the epitome of Mythological blindness, has entered a world where he can see clearly who people truly are, including Elphaba. This is the attitude Elphaba hoped would come from the Wizard, but it is Fiyero who has overcome the power of the Myth to grant Elphaba's deepest wish for acceptance.

This exchange between Elphaba and Fiyero takes place quickly and before we can digest the change in their relationship, the danger to Dr. Dillamond surfaces. Madame Morrible interrupts the class with several Ozian officials who forcibly remove Dr. Dillamond from the room. Madame Morrible explains that Animals are no longer permitted to teach, and as Dr. Dillamond is being carted off, he warns his students, "You're not being told the whole story! Remember that, class!" Then he is gone, replaced by a new professor, a dutiful soldier in the army of Myth.

Dr. Dillamond has been completely free of the Myth from the beginning of the musical. He occupies a unique position as a victim, and from that privileged position he sees more than anyone the truth of what has taken place. I say "privileged" because, although he is at risk of persecution, perhaps even death, he possesses the truth about good and evil. He is not a puppet like the rest, blindly following lies. He does not persecute others because he is all too aware of his own suffering to cause others to endure the same. He possesses what the writer and theologian James Alison calls the intelligence of the victim.[1] Fiyero has discovered it without being a victim himself. He was able to let go of his dependence on the Myth and find a new identity for himself, not as someone who is popular and happy because of deliberate blindness, but one who can accept his own flaws and mistakes, in particular the mistake he made about Elphaba. Rather than mindlessly believing the crowd's accusations that Elphaba is unlovable and unworthy of their attention, he can see things from her point of view. Rather than participate in her abuse, Fiyero will become Elphaba's champion and that of other potential victims of the Scapegoating Mechanism. James Alison says that someone with the intelligence of the victim can "tell the story of the lynching from the viewpoint of the victim's own understanding of what was going on, before the lynching, leading up to it, and during it."[2] Victims tell stories of persecution, not Myths.

ROMANTIC LOVE

The love story between Elphaba and Fiyero is very beautiful. Fiyero is the one who will heal Elphaba of her horrible self-image, helping her to see her most distinguishing characteristic, her green skin, in an entirely new way. It is a wonderful expression of the power of new love and the giddy experience that our lover knows and loves us unconditionally. But new love fades – take it from someone in her 27th year of marriage, the intensity doesn't last. Eventually, we begin to realize that our lover doesn't know us as well as we thought. There are miscommunications, failures to meet needs, hurt feelings – things that seemed impossible in the early days of passion. What has happened? Is the love over? Those who believe it is spend their lives in a series of relationships that they end abruptly as the blush of new love fades away. But romantic love must end in order for real love to take hold. Here's why.

In the first throws of romance, we love our lover because of how wonderful we feel when we're together. It's like a drug addiction and we can't get enough. Romantic love, as necessary and beautiful as it is, contains an element of the Mythological – I am in love with you more for the way you make me feel than for who you truly are. When romantic love fades, the real lover emerges with all their needs and flaws, annoying habits and petty grievances. Can we still love them? Was our love dependent on what they could do for us and not on whom they really were? That is the test that faces all couples when "the honeymoon is over." If the relationship ends at that point, then the romance wasn't based on anything more real than mutual thrill-seeking.

But sometimes the romance fades and leaves behind a tiny seed of true love. The romantic love was merely an appetizer, a lure to draw you into a relationship with someone who is worthy of being loved without strings attached. That's the possibility that Fiyero represents for Elphaba. As is true of real love, their relationship will demand much from them in terms of sacrifice and suffering, but we will cheer them on, hoping for a truly happy ending.

Both Dr. Dillamond and Fiyero represent for us what it is to be completely free of the Myth. Such a position is not without its dangers – both characters suffer persecution at the hands of the powerful. But rather than the cartoonish goodness that is found in the heroes of Myth, they epitomize the true goodness of the non-Mythological – a willingness to put the needs of others ahead of their own. Dr. Dillamond has continued to teach and bear witness to the true nature of Animals by speaking eloquently in class. He feels a loyalty to his students and to his fellow Animals, so rather than go into hiding to protect himself, he remains a vocal, visible, and therefore vulnerable, presence. Heroes of non-Mythological stories are not necessarily handsome – Dr. Dillamond is a goat, for heaven's sake – they don't need to wear white, and don't always get the prettiest girl. Non-mythological heroes are often perceived by the Myth as losers and are prone to being killed by the forces of the Sacrificial System. In Myth, heroes always come out winners. In non-Myth, heroes may die unglorified, shameful deaths.

Like Dr. Dillamond, Elphaba occupies the privileged position of victim, but her blindness is not yet cured. Her struggle is reminiscent of a butterfly caught in a spider's web: she knows she is in danger and being held in a trap against her will, but the harder she struggles the more entangled she becomes. Elphaba can see this much – she has never been taken in by the false accusations leveled against the Animals in general and Dr. Dillamond in particular. From the beginning, she has been able to see the innocence of this scapegoated victim, but she has fallen into the classic trap of those who are awakening to the truth. Rather than rejecting her role as victim, Elphaba has assumed a victim identity.

What do I mean by that? I'll begin my explanation with a personal story. When I was first married it was the early 1980's and the women's liberation movement was a fixture of popular culture. I was surrounded everywhere by the news that as a woman I was a victim of masculine oppression. I believed it. I felt oppressed and misunderstood and I took it out on my husband. You can hardly imagine the tongue-lashings he received for being a white male, oblivious to yet responsible for all the harm he and his kind had caused to womankind since the beginning of time. The women's lib movement was also sending me a message about how I needed to respond to this oppression – I needed to strive and succeed in the world dominated by men. I needed to get a job, receive high wages and quick promotions, keep my finances separate from my husband's and generally accept that any feminine or maternal instinct I felt had to be quashed in order for me to be liberated. In other words, I had to beat men at their own game by becoming a better man than they were.

The problem was that I didn't want a corporate job or a high salary or a prestigious promotion. I wanted to be a stay-at-home mom. I did stay at home to raise my children, but throughout those early years of motherhood I felt guilty, inadequate and humiliated about my choice. At parties, I apologized for being only a mom and with my husband I was weepy and needy, constantly in need of reassurance that I had some value as a human being.

What happened to me? The truth is that we are part of a patriarchal culture and as such, women have been victims of oppression. As a woman, I was in a unique position to perceive how oppression, and particularly the scapegoating mechanism, occurs. But I didn't understand how completely I had internalized the patriarchal view of women as inferior to men. I had adopted the culture's view of myself as inferior even though I knew it wasn't true. It was a real paradox – I knew I wasn't inferior, but I felt as if I was. My head told me one thing and my heart another. I could see only one way out – convince the patriarchy to change their opinion, and my husband, as accidental representative of the culture that had so wounded my sense of self, was the unlucky target of my efforts. I was locked in a dangerous tango with my oppressors, rejecting the patriarchal world and dependent on it at the same time. Why? Because I would never feel truly good about myself until I convinced the patriarchy of it. I needed to see my worth as a human being reflected back to me not only in my husband's loving gaze, but also from the entire world of men.

During those years I was at risk of becoming one of those stereotypical "angry feminists" that comics love to skewer. The anger is an expression of a grasping after something that is being withheld – an approval, love perhaps – from the oppressor. I was in danger of becoming a victim who was dependent on her victimizer to be healed.

All victims are at risk of falling into this trap. They need desperately to prove to themselves that what their oppressor has said about them is not true, but the proof must come from their oppressors. That is a victim identity in a nutshell – a victim locked in combat with their victimizer over possession of the ultimate prize, a sense of self-worth. The victim wants it and believes the victimizer has it to give. The big problem which I'm sure you can see is that the victimizer, whether an individual or an entire culture, cannot hold my self-worth ransom. It does not possess it and never will. My sense of self-worth is mine and mine alone. It can be wounded, hurt, kicked and bruised, but it can never belong to another and so I need never fight to get it back.

Elphaba can't see this yet, though we can see it for her. She is dependent on the Wizard, the representative of the people of Oz who have so rejected and wounded her, to be healed. Her heart's desire is for the Wonderful Wizard to recognize her for who she truly is and cure her of her handicap, the greenness that she has come to loath in herself. And so, like the feminists, Elphaba exhibits fits of rage that she does not completely understand and is unable to control.

After Dr. Dillamond is removed from the classroom, a new professor takes his place (his dress and make-up suggest a German Nazi officer). He shows the class a caged lion cub as an example of "the Silence of Progress." He explains that cages have been invented to prevent animals from ever learning how to speak, the implication being that talking Animals are an abomination and a threat. The tiny animal is trembling with fear and the sight of such suffering causes Elphaba to explode with another demonstration of her so-called magical power. This occurred earlier, when Madame Morrible took Nessarose away from Elphaba's care and into her own. Elphaba flew into a rage and Nessa's chair was magically drawn out of Morrible's hands back towards Elphaba. That anger was born of her own need for her father's approval and the possibility of failing her promise to him to care for Nessa. This time her anger is aroused out of her self-identification with the cub's suffering.

Anger seems to trigger these displays, and though no one actually gets hurt, they are out-of-control excesses, like a child's temper tantrum. As Elphaba's arms and legs flail about and angry tears blind her eyes, there may be no intent to harm anyone, but her powers are undisciplined and frightening. Her compassion is real, but because she is trapped in a victim identity and entangled with her oppressor, she does not know how to react in a way that does not mirror the very thing she is opposing. This display of raw power sends a message to her opponents that she is more like them than she would admit to herself. Elphaba is willing to play by their rules – she is willing to use violence to achieve her ends. This is what Morrible sees in that opening scene when she invites Elphaba into her sorcery class. Elphaba is a passionate person who can be molded to suit Morrible's – and the Wizard's – needs.

This is a chaotic scene, with Elphaba's rage confusing everyone, but Fiyero sees through the confusion. Without hesitation, he grabs the cage of the frightened lion cub, aligning himself with Elphaba in this one gesture. Fiyero's reaction to the injustice is one of clear-headed understanding. He is not paralyzed with rage, and in fact, he never shows the slightest sign of fear or anger. His response is elegant – he simply steps in and, without hurting anyone, saves the lion cub from its fate.

Elphaba now sees Fiyero as someone she could love. He understands the injustice that is being perpetrated in Oz and he has taken her side! He is intelligent and compassionate, a man of action yet one whose methods do not include the undisciplined rage that is so far Elphaba's only response to injustice. He is truly free, a man with the knowledge of who and what he is without needing confirmation from others. But because Elphaba is still convinced of the inherent unlovability of being green, she believes that Galinda is the girl he wants. In a tender song, Elphaba mourns the world's opinion of her:

> Hands touch, eyes meet
> Sudden silence, sudden heat
> Hearts leap in a giddy whirl
> He could be that boy
> But I'm not that girl
>
> Don't dream too far
> Don't lose sight of who you are

Don't remember that rush of joy
He could be that boy
I'm not that girl

What does she mean when she warns herself not to "lose sight of who you are"? I am afraid that this is one more example of how Elphaba, try as she might, cannot reject the ways of a world that is cruel to her. She seems to believe that there is some merit in the way the world values Galinda's blond curls and devalues her greenness. She trusts the world too much.

As her magical powers demonstrate, she cannot control her outbursts of hatred and violence. She is caught up in her compassion for the Animals and is determined to find out who is behind their suffering. What will she do when she discovers who it is? I believe she hopes that the Wizard will take care of it for her, that he will destroy whoever is victimizing the Animals. This is a sanctioning of violence born of her hatred for an enemy she has yet to identify.

It is worth making the argument here that whoever is behind the scapegoating of the Animals is truly bad and deserves whatever they get. Isn't that what this musical has been about, after all, trying to identify who is truly wicked so that we can rid ourselves of them once and for all? But before we jump to justifying our use of violence in this circumstance, the musical insists on offering us an uncomfortable comparison: If Elphaba uses the same methods of violence and hatred as her enemy, does her enemy win? To put the comparison another way, we have seen that someone is willing to use violence against the Animals. Is Elphaba any different if she is willing to use violence against that someone? The musical has already warned us with the song "What Is This Feeling?" that hatred obscures the difference between good and evil. In fact, Madame Morrible, who we will soon see serves the one who is responsible for silencing Dr. Dillamond, sees Elphaba not as an enemy but as a kindred spirit. Let us watch as the action unfolds.

Morrible has been in communication with the Wizard. In the next scene, Morrible informs Elphaba that the Wizard wishes to see her and Elphaba is delighted. All of her dreams are about to come true. Not only will she be able to help Dr. Dillamond, but Elphaba believes she will be transformed from an outcast into a true insider. From one without power, she will be acclaimed by the most powerful person in Oz. And her most secret and treasured dream of all – that the Wizard will "degreenify" her and people will see her for who she truly is – is now within reach. Elphaba wastes no time heading for the train station to begin her journey.

Galinda is someone who is so accomplished in the ways of the Sacrificial System that she knows it's all a sham. It's more like a game show than reality, more like reality TV than real life. She knows that a stage is set, people are assigned parts, the rules are handed out on Xeroxed copies for all to read and the winner is the one who most creatively applies the rules. Her very expertise is what will allow her eyes to be open to the truth concealed by Myth. But she is not there yet. She does, however, have the most perfect Galinda-esque advice for Elphaba – she says, "Remember, eye contact. And don't forget to tell him how wonderful he is. Wizards love that! And be yourself ... well, within reason."

Galinda may be all about playing by the Mythological Rules, but she seems to have an excellent grasp of what you can expect from people who derive their power from doing just that. She warns Elphaba not to be herself – don't be truthful about who you are – because this meeting with the Wizard will not be about who anyone truly is. Galinda knows better than anyone the futility of Elphaba's dream of being accepted by the Wizard.

Nessarose and Boq have come to the train station to say good-bye. Here's what happens:

NESSAROSE:
(Boq wheels Nessarose onstage.)
Elphaba! I'm so proud of you. I know father would be too.
We're all proud, aren't we?

ELPHABA:
You'll be alright, without me?

GALINDA:
She'll be fine! Bick will keep her company. Won't ya, Bick?

BOQ: ...It's Boq... And I can't do this anymore. (He exits.)

NESSAROSE:
Boq...!

GALINDA:
Nessa, maybe he just isn't the right one. For you.

NESSAROSE:
No, he's the one. It's me that's not right. Don't worry about me, Elphaba. I'll be fine. Safe journey. (She wheels herself offstage.)

Boq and Nessarose are still tragically under the spell of Myth. Boq's gesture of inviting Nessarose to the dance has not produced any real emotion within him. He is still caught up in his infatuation for Galinda even though the evidence continues to pile up that she is an unattainable object for him. And Nessa is still entangled by her desire for Boq, even though the evidence continues to pile up that he is an unattainable object for her. Yet, both are convinced that their happiness depends on acquiring that elusive love. They are both grasping for something they cannot have and the musical will reveal the tragic outcomes of their grasping desires.

Galinda expresses the unfortunate turn her own desires for Fiyero have taken. She tells Elphaba that he is "distant, and moodified, and he's been thinking, which really worries me. I never knew he cared so much about that old goat." When Fiyero shows up on the train platform, he tells Elphaba that he has been thinking a lot about the lion cub and Elphaba tells him that she has, too. Galinda, in an attempt to please Fiyero, quickly decides on an outward sign of how deeply she cares about the lion cub and Dr. Dillamond. She will change her name to reflect the funny way Dr. Dillamond pronounced it. From now on she will be Glinda, without the "Ga." This is a false gesture on her part, but we wonder if it might yield results anyway. We can remember the wonderful transformation brought about by the gift of the black hat. Perhaps trying on a new identity is a first step to acquiring one.

But Fiyero is unimpressed and unconvinced that "Glinda" shares his and Elphaba's compassion. Remember, his belief in outward signs and appearances has been shattered. He runs off and Elphaba turns to Glinda:

> ELPHABA:
> Galinda …
>
> GLINDA:
> It's Glinda now. Stupid idea, I don't even know what made me say it.
>
> ELPHABA:
> It doesn't matter what your name is – everyone loves you!
>
> GLINDA:
> I don't care! I want him. I don't even think he's perfect anymore and I still want him. This must be what other people feel like. How do they bear it? (They embrace.)

There is a tension here for the audience. We suspect that Fiyero has fallen out of love with Glinda and that the two friends are now rivals for Fiyero's love. But Elphaba doesn't believe she has a chance with Fiyero, so she surrenders before the battle even begins. And what chance does she have if Glinda begins to become less of a Barbie doll and more like a real human being? From her last comment, it seems possible that Glinda is capable of loving someone for who they are, imperfections and all. Elphaba seizes on that hope and immediately asks Glinda to come with her to the Emerald City.

Glinda accepts, saying she's always wanted to see the city and they sing a fun-filled song together. By the end of the song they are at the gates of the Wizard's palace in a most marvelous mood. Glinda is impressed by the glitter, the dress salons and palaces. And Elphaba can't believe all the libraries and museums and that everything is green! She says, "I want to remember this moment. Always. Nobody's staring. Nobody's pointing. For the first time, I'm somewhere ... where I belong."

Of course, that is all anyone wants. Both Elphaba and Glinda want to be popular, to be accepted and to know they are loved. But what price are they willing to pay for such love? The Myth claims that there is no price too steep to pay for such a lofty personal goal. Remember the Creed of Self-Worship?

- I believe in one god – myself.
- The fulfillment of my desires is the ultimate good.
- Anyone or anything that gets in the way of the fulfillment of my desires is my enemy and is subject to destruction by any means available.

This is the creed of the Emerald City and of the Wizard himself, which the girls will find out soon enough. But Fiyero seems to have abandoned this creed for another one altogether. He has faced his own shallowness and no longer lives an unexamined life. Rather than "dancing through life" and putting his own happiness ahead of anyone else's, he has taken up the cause of the Animals, devoting his life to helping them. We are not sure what he is doing behind the scenes to help the Animals, but he does not go with the girls to see the Wizard. Does he know something they do not?

Though Fiyero may indeed be an object both Elphaba and Glinda desire, they have found another desire, one they do not have to compete over. Both desire to be in the Emerald City and it is big enough to contain both of them without conflict. In fact, by the end of the song, Elphaba sings that they are "two good friends" enjoying one wonderful day and Glinda corrects her with "two best friends." It is a beautiful moment of reconciliation. Seemingly, their animosities have been left behind at Shiz and they have come to admire, respect, and even love one another. But this brief moment of unity between Elphaba and Glinda is about to be shattered. An Ozian Official announces, "The Wizard will see you now!" All their dreams will be tested in the corridors of the powerful Wizard of Oz. As the scene comes to a close, the words of Dr. Dillamond echo in our heads, "You're not being told the whole story. Remember that, class!"

9

Defying Gravity

The thing is, my green girlie, it's not for a girl, or a student, or a citizen to assess what is wrong. This is the job of the leaders, and why we exist.

MAGUIRE, *Wicked*

The world wants to be deceived.

SEBASTIAN BRANT (1457–1521), *The Ship of Fools*

It is hard to fight an enemy who has outposts in your head.

SALLY KEMPTON

Grand, green, exquisite. The Emerald City is everything Elphaba and Glinda thought it would be – a city where dreams come true, full of opportunities and welcoming to the popular and alienated alike. Elphaba finally feels that this is a place where she belongs, and for a fleeting moment is at peace with her greenness. Any lingering doubts or resentments the girls had toward each other have melted away on the streets of this city of hope and love. Hope. Love. Peace. These are not just promises the city makes, they are the realities Elphaba and Glinda see as they promise each other that though this is to be a visit of only one day, they will return and make this city their home. It is perfect! Who wouldn't want to spend their whole lives here? But the peace of the Emerald City is a peace acquired by following the Mythological Rules and we know that this joy the girls feel cannot last.

It is time to meet the Wizard, and both Elphaba and Glinda feel confident that once the Wizard knows what happened to Dr. Dillamond and the Animals he will make it all better. Though both girls have broken free in small ways, they are still under the spell of the Myth and its definition of good and evil. When they see the Emerald City first hand, their false confidence is bolstered. They reason that only a truly good Wizard could rule over such an amazing city. Surely their meeting will be only a formality. They will share what they know with the Wizard and leave it to him to save the Animals. At home, they will tell everyone of their adventure and dream of returning to this amazing place, confident that whatever was wrong in Oz will be made right in a hurry.

But within seconds, their expectations are upended. A large mechanical head with an inhumanly loud voice booms, "I am Oz, the Great and Terrible! Who are you and why do you seek me?" Elphaba is speechless until Glinda prompts her to say something. She stutters, "Uh ... Elphaba Thropp, your terribleness!" At this point, a man climbs out from behind the mechanical head and shows them that he is the real Wizard, not the contraption. He explains, that the head is just for show because, "People expect this sort of thing and you have to give people what they want."

The Wizard begins his song and I think it a stroke of genius that Schwartz and Holzman paint the Wizard as a song-and-dance man. He attempts to deceive the girls with his consoling words, to comfort them with a sweet song so that his version of the truth will not be questioned. He claims to have Elphaba's best interest at heart, like a father toward a daughter. In spite of Elphaba's history with Frex, she still believes the Wizard, and so begins to explain that she and Glinda are here "because something bad is happening ..."

Before she can finish, the Wizard assures her that he knows why they have come. He seems willing to help them, but there are strings attached. They must first prove themselves worthy of his help. He actually wants to test Elphaba's "adeptness," though at what he doesn't say.

Of course, after having been through the misguided attempts at relationships that have plagued this musical so far, we are cautious when we hear of the Wizard's conditional response. Haven't people been abusive and manipulative of each other throughout the musical so far? Galinda used Boq, Boq used Nessarose, and Galinda and Elphaba competed to become Morrible's favorite student. But surely the Wizard does not succumb to these petty resentments. Surely the Wizard is capable of genuine relationships rooted in generosity. He does not use people for personal gain. Not the Wonderful Wizard of Oz.

But that is exactly what and who the Wonderful Wizard is. We are shocked to find out that Madame Morrible is there with the Wizard, as his press secretary. She explains quite plainly how the Wizard's generosity works, and she puts it forward as a virtue. She says, "If you do something for him, he'll do much for you." That, as we know, is the definition of generosity in the Emerald City.

The Wizard lives by the Creed of the Sacrificial System: he himself is the god he worships, his desires are supreme, and anyone who opposes him is his enemy. Of course, the Wizard is as good as God to everyone in the Land of Oz, so not only does he believe that his desires represent the ultimate good for himself, he believes they represent the ultimate good for all of Oz. And the Ozians, for their part, believe him. So anyone who gets in the way of the will of the Wizard is the enemy of all of Oz and must be truly wicked. Conversely, anyone who advances the will of the Wizard is a friend of Oz and must be truly good. Good and wicked are easily identified in this system: The test is whether or not the person's desires are aligned with those of the Wizard.

Just as victims within the Sacrificial System are vulnerable to falling into certain self-defeating traps, so are the truly good, the gods of the land. Of course, it is only from within the Myth that they are heroes, great and powerful leaders, beneficent rulers who want only what is best for their people. From outside the Myth, from the perspective of those who possess the knowledge of the victim, they can be viewed as oppressors.

Tragically, the very people who want to do the most good often end up, within the Myth, doing the most evil. They are the successful ones who, like the Wizard and Glinda, are masters of the Mythological rules. In fact, the Wizard explains how scapegoating works: "Where I come from, everyone knows the best way to bring people together is to give them a good enemy." The Wizard and leaders like him owe their success within the Sacrificial System to their utter and complete belief that everything they do is by definition good. Even using scapegoating to preserve their own power becomes an exercise in goodness because of their belief that they know what's best for their people. They are often startled and deeply offended by accusations of wrongdoing, because they believe in the goodness of their own morality with all their hearts.

It's an interesting paradox – a beneficent leader who can justify deceit in the name of good. I came across a startling example of this in an account of the trial of a wartime leader of the Bosnian Serbs named Momcilo Krajisnik. The newspaper reported, "Prosecutors said that one of [Krajisnik's] main functions was to coordinate and oversee the brutal ethnic separation campaign carried out in 37 Bosnian townships. Judges found him guilty of deportations, forced transfers and persecution as well as murder and extermination of Croats and Bosnian Muslims."[1] One might imagine that he was a monstrous human being, someone who could be easily recognized by us and even by himself as evil. Yet a few paragraphs later the reporter made this observation: "Mr. Krajisnik testified for weeks in his own defense, claiming he was unaware of any crimes and instead was a peacemaker."[2]

Was he just trying to con the judge, or did he truly believe in himself as a peacemaker? If his defense was more than a con job, then it could stand to reason that the judge had made a terrible mistake. I used to read articles like this and my head would spin – both sides of the story couldn't be true, I thought. Either he is truly guilty or the judge made a mistake and found an innocent man guilty of a crime he didn't commit. But that reasoning is square within the Myth. Standing outside the Myth, I can see how both things can be true – someone can be guilty of terrible crimes all the while claiming that he is a peacemaker. It is possible because within the Myth the formula for peace includes violence. According to Rule #3, violence can be good if good people are using it against bad people. We can see behind Krajisnik's comment his belief in his own goodness as well as his confidence that he had located evil in his victims, Croats and Bosnian Muslims. Again, it is only we who stand outside Krajisnik's Mythological world who can see them as victims. To Krajisnik they were no doubt evil enemies who had to be destroyed to protect himself and the other good people like him.

Why can we clearly see the innocence of Krajisnik's victims when he cannot? For the same reason we can see the innocence of Dr. Dillamond and the Wizard cannot. Because these victims are their scapegoats, not ours. We are blind to our own scapegoats, but not to the scapegoats of others. It is why we need trusted friends and a courageous community dedicated to truth that can constantly call us on our accusations of evil and the actions that follow. The same Mythological trap that has enmeshed the Wizard and Krajisnik can catch us, too, if we are not vigilant. Within the Myth, adversaries on all sides can claim the mantle of goodness with complete confidence and conviction. After all, according to the rules of Myth, they *are* good.

Up to this point in the musical, Elphaba cannot imagine that the Wizard is not the paragon of goodness she hoped and needed him to be. When he says she must pass a test, she eagerly asks what he wants her to do. He produces a book called the Grimmerie. It is a book of spells written in a lost language that even Morrible, the Mistress of Sorcery, has trouble reading. But the Wizard explains that "It's a kind of recipe book for change," and he wants Elphaba to read it in order to give his monkey servant, Chistery, the ability to fly. For his own good, of course. The monkey "watches the birds so longingly every morning" that the Wizard's tender heart was moved to help him fulfill his desire.

The Wizard and Morrible think Elphaba can read this ancient language because she has demonstrated exceptional, though undisciplined, powers. Naturally, they hope to mold her abilities to suit their own purposes. Elphaba reads the words easily, and no sooner does she begin chanting than Chistery begins to change. He seems to be in pain and Elphaba grows alarmed. She wants to go back, to reverse what is happening but is told by Morrible that the spells are irreversible. Then Morrible says to the Wizard, "I knew she had the power. I told you!" Elphaba understands now that the Wizard and Morrible had planned all along to get her to the Emerald City, using her compassion for Dr. Dillamond as a way to trick her into thinking it was her idea. She is shocked, but Morrible says, "For you, too, dearie! You benefit, too." It is all about personal gain, of course, and fulfilling your own desires.

Finally, the ugly truth is revealed and Elphaba understands. The Wizard wants to use flying monkeys as spies so they can "fly around Oz" and "report any subversive Animal activity." The Grimmerie is the user's manual to the Sacrificial System. It produces change all right, but is a recipe for how to change conflict into peace by choosing scapegoats. It is the sacred text for the individuals who believe that violence can be an instrument of peace, people like the Wizard and Krajinsik. Its spells allow you to change people into objects that can be used, manipulated, and destroyed, and its methods are responsible for the false hope, love, and peace of the Emerald City. Sadly, the spells it casts are irreversible when they lead to the victim's death. By using her powers to read the book for the Wizard, Elphaba would be strengthening the Wizard's ruthless effort to maintain control over Oz.

The Animals, of course, are no real threat to the Wizard. They have no army or plans for conquest of the Emerald City. It is because they cannot defend themselves the Wizard has chosen them as enemies. Exactly because no one will rise to their defense – except Elphaba – the Wizard can destroy the Animals without fear of inciting unrest or an armed retaliation. And when anything goes wrong in the city or the land, the Wizard can blame them. Because the Animals have been chosen as scapegoats, however, they know better than any what is going on. So the Wizard has actually created a true enemy to his power, a group who can cause his kingdom to crumble simply by telling the truth. Where at first he had simply chosen a victim that no one would defend, by allowing the Animals to see the truth of the system he has now created the instrument of his own demise, escalating his drive to exterminate them.

Horrified by all this, Elphaba says to the Wizard, "You can't read this book at all, can you? That's why you need an enemy. And spies. And

WHEN ROLE MODELS FALL

When I was a sophomore in high school, I ran for school secretary. Not the most ambitious office, but as you know, I was not like Glinda and running for any office was an act of courage. There were a few girls, nerdy and uncool like myself, who liked me enough to want to run my campaign. They made posters and put them around the school, wore homemade pins with my name on them, and were hopeful about my chances.

The day of the election we voted in actual voting booths, the kind where a curtain closed behind you and to vote you pulled the lever next to your candidate's name. Tallies appeared mechanically on a back panel and were read by the election officials. Surprisingly, in the school assembly that afternoon, my name was called as the winner. There was a smattering of applause, not loud enough to represent a winning majority and I wondered if the others who had voted for me simply didn't have the energy to clap.

As I was about to board the bus home, I was summoned back inside to the principal's office where I was told that a mistake had been made reading the results. A number had been transposed and I hadn't actually won. I had lost. My opponent, a popular girl who wasn't an honor roll student at all, had won and was the students' choice to be secretary. I was devastated, not as much by the loss as by the humiliation that I would suffer when the truth was known. But the school principal offered me a way out. She said that if I wanted her to, she and the teacher who recorded the results wouldn't tell anyone about the mistake. At that point, only the three of us knew the truth, so it was really up to me. She'd do whatever I wanted.

I couldn't believe Sister Margaret (not her real name) would propose such a deceit. I refused her offer, but my faith in her character was shaken. Like Elphaba, I had discovered that someone whom I admired was frail and flawed, like all human beings. I'm sure she was trying to save me the taste

...continued on next page

...continued from previous page

of humiliation that the mistake had caused, but such tender motives were no excuse for falsifying an election, no matter how minor in the history of democracy.

We all have tales to tell of times when someone we trusted has let us down. Such disappointments are inevitable and the temptation within the Myth is to demonize them – once seen as completely good, now they become completely evil. The truth is, they were and are neither. Politicians, religious leaders, corporate CEO's, artists, writers and movie stars – people we put up on pedestals and idolize as if they were gods and goddesses – are no such thing at all. They are as human as you and I. To expect otherwise, to ricochet from idolatry to condemnation because we discover they are human is cruel and unjust, and it deprives us of the lessons they have to offer. The Myth wants us to be blinded by extremes on both ends of the spectrum. But we must insist on keeping our eyes wide open, allowing both our idols and our villains to be what they truly are: human.

cages. You have no real power!" She sees the truth behind the Sacrificial Mechanism now. The "power" of those who use it is the same power that makes Glinda popular – it is the ability to manipulate public opinion. Elphaba sees for the first time that the Wizard's moral claim of goodness is a lie so convincing even he believes it. His inability to read the Grimmerie is like the metaphor of blindness we have seen before – those under the spell of the Myth, even those who have perfected its use, do not understand that what the Myth calls good is actually evil. They have fallen so deeply into the trap that all they see is darkness, unaware that the light of truth is within their reach.

Though Elphaba has seen a glimmer of truth, she is not able to free herself from her conflict with the Wizard. Rather than define herself as she had done before by trying to please the Wizard, she will now define herself in opposition to him. "The Wizard and I" becomes "Not-the-

Wizard, that's me." She rejects the Wizard, refusing to participate in his plan of persecution of the Animals, and so she becomes an enemy of Oz. Morrible calls the guards as Elphaba tries to make her escape and the Wizard climbs back inside the mechanical head.

Now we see the Myth-making power of the Sacrificial Mechanism fully revealed. As Glinda and Elphaba race up the stairs to flee from the guards, Morrible proclaims:

> Citizens of Oz! There is an enemy who must be found and captured! Believe nothing she says. She's evil. Responsible for the mutilation of these poor, innocent monkeys! Her green skin is but an outward manifestation of her twisted nature! This distortion – this repulsion – this – Wicked Witch!!!!!!!!!!!!

Remember, she is the press secretary! And a good one, indeed! The citizens of Oz have agreed, through their unquestioning loyalty to the Wizard, to allow the Animals to be sacrificed for the peace. They will turn a blind eye to the violence and believe in the lies the Wizard tells them, because the results are so wonderful – a marvelous green city that welcomes everyone and makes your dreams come true. Unless, of course, you are the chosen scapegoat. Then the Emerald City is a city of horrors, not a city of peace at all, but a ruthless, heartless place that is blind to the suffering it causes its most vulnerable inhabitants.

Let's see how Elphaba responds to her discovery about the Wizard. We are now at the final scene of Act One and a major turning point for both Glinda and Elphaba. They may not fully understand the depth of the lie being told by the Myth, but they do see the truth about the Wizard. How will they respond to the revelation that it was the Wizard himself who had Dr. Dillamond fired, the Wizard himself who has ordered the Animals caged and silenced? This knowledge turns their world upside down with the power of a cyclone. In an attempt to restore a sense of calm and peace, the girls use the tools they know well, those of the Sacrificial System. They revert to their previous relationship of being mirror images of one another's anger and resentment. They sing parallel lyrics. Listen:

GLINDA:
(Spoken) *Elphaba, why couldn't you have stayed calm for once, instead of flying off the handle!*
(Sung) I hope you're happy
I hope you're happy now
I hope you're happy how you
Hurt your cause forever
I hope you think you're clever

ELPHABA:
I hope you're happy
I hope you're happy too
I hope you're proud how you
Would grovel in submission
To feed your own ambition

BOTH:
So though I can't imagine how
I hope you're happy right now...

Because they disagree on just how evil the Wizard is they find themselves opposed to each other once again. Glinda still wants to be part of the Wizard's administration, but Elphaba has now totally rejected the Wizard and everything for which he stands. Such opposition feels familiar and right and we wonder if they have landed back in these positions to stay. Where earlier they sang of their loathing for one another, now their song trembles with rage. Just as hatred reduced them to reflections of each other, now anger does the same thing. They sing almost the same words and the anger in their voices is indistinguishable. Neither girl is happy.

Elphaba tries to explain that everything has changed for her. There is no way to go back to the old dream of being with the Wizard and finding a fairy tale ending for her and for Dr. Dillamond. She says she's "through with playing by the rules of someone else's game." Listen to her lament:

Too late for second-guessing
Too late to go back to sleep
It's time to trust my instincts
Close my eyes and leap

It's time to try
Defying gravity
I think I'll try
Defying gravity
And you can't pull me down...

GLINDA:
Can't I make you understand, you're
Having delusions of grandeur...?

ELPHABA:
I'm through accepting limits
'Cuz someone says they're so
Some things I cannot change
But till I try, I'll never know
Too long I've been afraid of
Losing love I guess I've lost
Well, if that's love
It comes at much too high a cost
I'd sooner buy
Defying gravity
Kiss me goodbye
I'm defying gravity
And you can't pull me down...

Elphaba understands that the people who claimed to love her, from her father to Morrible to the Wizard, were not acting in her best interests at all. What they wanted was her silent agreement to obey their will, not hers, to play by the rules of their game. It's the game that has no limits, that permits the use and abuse of another to achieve the fulfillment of your own desires. But Elphaba doesn't want to play their game anymore; she especially doesn't want to be abused. Rather than attempting to be just like her father or Nessa, she will now choose to be their exact opposites. Elphaba adopts an identity of opposition – her own goodness defined in contrast to the wickedness of those around her. Her moral standing is defined by whom she is *not* – she is not the Wizard, not Frex, not Nessarose, not Morrible or Glinda.

She knows now that she needn't be afraid of losing their love – it wasn't true love anyway. Their love has kept her down and she will no longer play by their rules, which are the rules of abuse advocated by the Myth. "Defying gravity" is her way of expressing her "no." "Gravity" expresses how we feel trapped inside those rules, how the Myth convinces us that there are no alternatives to its way of doing things. Defying the Myth, we are led to believe, is as futile as defying gravity.

Glinda and Elphaba each attempt to convince the other she is wrong. Glinda wants Elphaba to apologize to the Wizard. Elphaba wants Glinda to ride away with her on the broomstick that now floats and flies like Chistery. Elphaba has used the levitation spell on the broom and is ready to fly away. She is intoxicated by her growing mastery of the Sacrificial System. Despite her claim that she will defy the system, she remains trapped within it. She tells Glinda that they have the potential to do wonderful things together, that there are no limits to what they can do – a claim that can only be made from within the Myth.

ELPHABA:
Unlimited
Together we're unlimited
Together we'll be the greatest team there's ever been
Glinda –
Dreams the way we planned 'em

GLINDA:
If we work in tandem...

BOTH:
There's no fight we cannot win
Just you and I
Defying gravity
With you and I
Defying gravity

ELPHABA:
They'll never bring us down...

Elphaba is caught in a spiraling rivalry with the Wizard in which he feels justified to use any means to defeat Elphaba, and Elphaba feels the same. It is a destructive duel that may not end until one has destroyed the other. But Glinda can't oppose the Wizard, at least not this way – not in anger, not with an uncontrolled hatred. Her refusal is a tender one. She drapes a cape around Elphaba's shoulders and they sing in a different tone now, one of regret and genuine love, wishing each other the best on the path they have chosen.

GLINDA:
(Spoken) *Elphie, you're trembling... Here, put this around you...*
(She drapes a black cape around her.)
(Sung) I hope you're happy
Now that you're choosing this...

ELPHABA:
You too – I hope it brings you bliss

BOTH:
I really hope you get it
And you don't live to regret it
I hope you're happy in the end
I hope you're happy, my friend...

What neither the audience nor Glinda knows is exactly what Elphaba plans to do. We guess that she is going to help the Animals in any way she can. She has chosen to oppose the Wizard, which appears to be the right choice. He is causing terrible harm to the Animals and the peace he has brought to Oz is built upon lies. But Elphaba is using the language of one-upmanship towards her enemy that we saw in the loathing scene between Elphaba and Galinda. Elphaba is determined to defy gravity so that no one will ever bring her down again, literally and figuratively. She will ride that seesaw high enough so that she will be undefeatable. She even sends a direct challenge to the Wizard.

> To those who'd ground me,
> Take a message back from me!
> Tell them how I am defying gravity!!!
> I'm flying high defying gravity!!!
> And soon I'll match them in renown
> And nobody
> In all of Oz...
> No wizard that there is or was
> Is ever gonna bring
> Me down!!!

When Elphaba sings, "And soon I'll match them in renown" we know that she has not rejected the rules of the game that the Wizard is playing. Just as she and Glinda had become mirror images of each through hatred and anger, now the differences between Elphaba and the Wizard have dissolved. Sure, one claims to want to destroy the Animals and one wants to help them, but they are using the same means – the willingness to destroy their enemy – to achieve their goals. Rather than reject methods of violence, Elphaba firmly believes that her violence is good, while the Wizard's is bad. Elphaba has not set her feet on a path out of the Sacrificial System, but on one leading her deeper into its dark and deadly forest.

Elphaba has found the courage to see that the Wizard's wonderfulness is nothing but a lie, but does she have the courage to see that he is lying about other things as well? Will she ever understand that he is wrong about his methods – that no happiness and nothing good can come of trying to destroy another? Will she discover another way to help the Animals and Chistery, one that will defeat the Wizard's plan without succumbing to his wicked methods?

As Act One closes, we fear for Elphaba's life. But we fear for her soul as well.

10

Thank Goodness

Fear is the main source of superstition, and one of the main sources of cruelty. To conquer fear is the beginning of wisdom.

BERTRAND RUSSELL, British author, mathematician, & philosopher (1872 – 1970)

To be without some of the things you want is an indispensable part of happiness.

BERTRAND RUSSELL (1872-1970)

Sometimes the measure of friendship isn't your ability to not harm but your capacity to forgive the things done to you and ask forgiveness for your own mistakes.

RANDY K. MILHOLLAND, *Something Positive*, Comic

Act Two opens with the realization of our worst fears. The Wizard has chosen Elphaba as his new scapegoat and offered her to the people to further conceal the truth of his wickedness. As audience members, we are frightened for the safety of our new friend, someone we have come to love and admire, faults and all. We know she is prone to fits of temper, that she can be as petty as Glinda, and that she doesn't love herself as much as we love her. But we can't help but admire her unflinching courage, her ability to stare head on at the truth even if it means the crumbling of everything she has believed in. Her idol has fallen and with him has fallen her belief in goodness itself.

Accepting the truth about the Wizard's culpability in the oppression of Dr. Dillamond and the Animals is a personal tragedy for Elphaba. The discovery that her adversary is the most powerful man in Oz means that it will be much more difficult to help Dr. Dillamond than she first thought. But she also realizes that her hopes for being loved and accepted by her family and all of Oz have vanished in a heartbeat. If the Wizard is not good, Elphaba cannot imagine how goodness can exist at all. She is disillusioned. As the action unfolds, we will see Elphaba vacillate between despair and desperate action. She despairs because she cannot imagine how, without a paragon of goodness like the Wizard, she can hope to be rehabilitated. She acts with courage on behalf of Dr. Dillamond when she refuses to cooperate with the Wizard. To save her friend, Chistery and the monkeys, and all the Animals of Oz, she has given up her dream of being loved.

Elphaba has adopted a victim identity, unable to believe in her own lovability until she sees it in the eyes of her oppressor. But is it possible that the Wizard can have a change of heart and give her the reflection of self-worth she needs to see? Can someone like the Wizard, who is so indebted to the Sacrificial System for power and prestige, ever give it up for the good of another? Looking to our world, we see little evidence to hope for such an outcome. We even have an adage that expresses the iron hold the Mythological world has on its inhabitants: *Absolute power corrupts absolutely*. This saying refers to Mythological power gained through use and abuse of victims and the methods of violence. It is the power of oppression that is grasped and accumulated through strict adherence to the Sacrificial System. Once you taste the benefits of power, you become addicted to it. It seems to deliver everything anyone could want – not just power, but wealth, happiness, friends, prestige and fame, even love. Where is the incentive for the Wizard to change?

The musical answers that question by offering us a peek inside the heart of Glinda the Good. Glinda is not the simple, one-dimensional character she first appeared to be when she entered the stage riding high on a trolley of trunks and suitcases surrounded by a clique of admiring friends. She has undergone a gradual transformation through the first act, and as Act Two opens, we will see her fears and doubts in what is my favorite song in the musical, "Thank Goodness."

Remember that Glinda also believed in the goodness of the Wizard. She believed in it as completely as Elphaba did, and her particular belief centered on the expected benefits of "being good" within the Sacrificial System. The Myth makes promises to its followers and Glinda believes in them. She is convinced that she will find happiness in a fairy tale ending, because everyone who is popular, powerful, and "good" gets the happy endings they deserve. If she plays by the rules, she believes she can expect big rewards. One of the primary rules of the Sacrificial System permits the use and abuse of others in pursuit of one's own happiness. And Glinda has gleefully done just that.

Let's turn to the opening scene of Act Two. We are at a public gathering that begins with the Ozians singing about their fear of the Wicked Witch.

OZIANS:
Ev'ry day, more wicked
Ev'ry day, the terror grows!
All of Oz is ever on alert!
That's the way with Wicked-
Spreading fear where e'er she goes
Seeking out new victims she can hurt!

A HYSTERICAL WOMAN:
Like some terrible green blizzard
Throughout the land she flies...

AN OUTRAGED MAN:
Defaming our poor Wizard
With her calumnies and lies!

OZIANS:
She lies!
Save us from the Wicked!
Shield us so we won't be hexed!
Give us warning:
Where will she strike next?
Where will she strike next?
Where will she strike next!?

What we know, however, is that it is the Wizard and his press secretary, Madame Morrible, who have been telling lies and slandering reputations, not Elphaba. They have successfully deflected attention from their own quite real wickedness onto Elphaba, and are now using her as a scapegoat. Elphaba's life is at risk and the tenor of the Ozian crowd reminds us of bloodthirsty lynch mobs.

Onto the scene steps Glinda with Fiyero and Morrible. Glinda is a witness to the fateful interview between Elphaba and the Wizard. She knows who is telling the truth and who is telling lies, and this knowledge has the potential to call everything she thought she knew and believed into question, especially her belief in happy endings. Rather than redoubling her efforts on behalf of victims, as Elphaba has done, Glinda retreats into the familiar world of Myth where her wishes and desires are always and forever the greatest good.

Glinda, with her belief in happy endings, has as little motive for change as does the Wizard. But Glinda has been spending a lot of time with someone who dwells in the shadows as a victim of the Mythological world. Her friendship with Elphaba has raised doubts within her, little whispering voices that she can't quite silence. Whenever we allow ourselves to hear the victim's story, their suffering can pierce the veil of lies told by the Myth. For Glinda, the murderous rage of the Ozians is monstrous proof that the little voices in her head are the voices of truth. But her wand is so magical, her gown so magnificent, and her rank so high, that Glinda cannot reconcile that all this glory can be wrong. She is not yet ready to give it all up, so she struggles to protect her friend and her own position within the Myth at the same time. Let's see how she manages.

Glinda's response to the mounting fury of the Ozians is perhaps one of the most cleverly insightful lines of the musical. "Fellow Ozians – as terrifying as terror is," she says, "let us put aside our panic for this one day ... and celebrate!" Glinda knows in her heart that if she wants to help Elphaba, she must persuade the people to let go of their panic. She must somehow undo the effects of the accusations made by Morrible and the Wizard. So she soothes them as she would a child who needs to be parted from a favorite toy. People like to be terrified. It is one way of knowing for sure what and where the wicked thing is – somewhere out there – so they can feel safe and secure right where they stand.

So Glinda proposes a distraction. She sings her suggestion that the gathered mob have a celebration instead of a lynching.

GLINDA:
Oh what a celebration
We'll have today

OZIANS:
Thank goodness!

GLINDA:
Let's have a celebration
The Glinda way ...

OZIANS:
Thank goodness!

MORRIBLE:
Fin'lly a day that's
Totally Wicked-Witch free!

ALL:
We couldn't be happier
Thank goodness!

THE ONLY THING WE HAVE TO FEAR IS FEAR ITSELF

In his first inaugural address, speaking to a nation in the grips of the worst economic depression in the nation's history, President Roosevelt had this to say:

> First of all, let me assert my firm belief that the only thing we have to fear is fear itself – nameless, unreasoning, unjustified terror which paralyzes needed efforts to convert retreat into advance.*

Is that really true? Is our own fear worse than any other threat we might face? At the time of Roosevelt's famous speech, the nation was facing the collapse of the economy, the banking system, and the government itself. Many believed that the United States was in its last days. It seemed there was plenty to fear, and justifiably so. But Roosevelt began his speech with a warning against fear. Rather than motivate people to follow his policies by frightening them, he appealed to their better natures. Here's what he said:

> If I read the temper of our people correctly, we now realize as we have never realized before our interdependence on each other; that we can not merely take but we must give as well; that if we are to go forward, we must move as a trained and loyal army willing to sacrifice for the good of a common discipline, because without such discipline no progress is made, no leadership becomes effective. We are, I know, ready and willing to submit our lives and property to such discipline, because it makes possible a leadership which aims at a larger good. This I propose to offer, pledging that the larger purposes will bind upon us all as a sacred obligation with a unity of duty hitherto evoked only in time of armed strife.**

How different from the Wizard and Morrible. Where they use fear to promote their policies, Roosevelt used

...continued on next page

...continued from previous page

reason. Where they use every violent and abusive means at their disposal, Roosevelt advocated discipline and restraint. Rather than whipping up a lynch mob, Roosevelt proposed an "army willing to sacrifice" for the good of that restraint. Roosevelt believed in a "larger good" beyond the immediate satisfaction of one's needs for security or power, and he perceived fear as the enemy of that good. Why?

As we see in Oz, fear clouds our reason and causes us to lash out blindly, creating enemies where we might find friends. Fear restricts our vision so that we protect our own narrow needs at the expense of everyone else's. Out of fear of the Witch, the Ozians willingly participate in her death and in the destruction of the Animals. Spending their energy on fighting imaginary enemies, the Ozians have no strength left to challenge their corrupt leaders or for the true work of discipline and self-sacrifice. What would our nation discover today if we examined our present fears? What discipline and self-sacrifice do our times demand of us?

* Franklin D. Roosevelt, 32nd President of U.S. 1882 – 1945. First Inaugural Address, 4 Mar, 1933.

** Ibid.

Glinda is inviting the Ozians to turn from their terror to celebrate her achievements. She has what she claimed she wanted: 1) She is a sorceress now named Glinda the Good, 2) She is fully established in the government as an advisor to the Wizard himself, and 3) She is engaged to Fiyero. Could anyone have acquired more desirable and good objects? If so, Glinda cannot imagine it. She sings of the fulfillment of the promise that by acquiring these things she will find happiness and she turns to Fiyero for affirmation:

GLINDA:
We couldn't be happier

Right dear?
Couldn't be happier
Right here
Look what we've got
A fairy tale plot
Our very own happy ending
Where we couldn't be happier
True dear?
Couldn't be happier
And we're happy to share our ending vicariously
With all of you!
He couldn't look handsomer
I couldn't be humbler
Because happy is what happens
When all your dreams come true ...

All of Glinda's dreams have come true, but they are not her dreams. Rather they are those of the Myth: get the wand, get the power, get the prince. Now Glinda wants to collect the big payoff. She wants, she expects as her due, happiness. But her assertions of happiness seem tinged with doubt. Glinda wants to celebrate the happiness that comes from the Sacrificial System, but she doesn't really feel happy deep inside.

The mob, however, does seem soothed. Madame Morrible, in her role as press secretary, begins the story of Glinda's "braverism." The mob listens like children hearing a favorite bedtime story as Morrible retells Glinda and Elphaba's meeting with the Wizard. But in Morrible's version, Glinda is the heroine and Elphaba an evil intruder, seeking only to disrupt and harm. The Ozians are aroused again, quickly taking up their part of the Myth-telling, creating lies about Elphaba that make her completely other, totally un-Ozian. In our world we would say, inhuman. They demonize her.

PEOPLE IN CROWD:
I hear she has an extra eye
That always remains awake!

I hear that she can shed her skin
As easily as a snake!
I hear some rebel animals
Are giving her food and shelter!
I hear her soul is so unclean
Pure water can melt her!

FIYERO:
What!?

OZIANS:
Melt her!?
Please – Somebody go and melt her!

The mob is spinning lies into truths at breakneck speed. Fiyero, who up till now has been playing his role as dutiful fiancé, cannot keep silent anymore.

FIYERO:
Well, I can't just stand here grinning pretending to go along with all of this!

GLINDA:
Do you think I like to hear them say those awful things about her? I hate it!

FIYERO:
Then what are we doing here? Let's go, let's get out of here!

GLINDA:
I can't, I can't leave now, when people are looking to me to raise their spirits.

FIYERO:
You can't leave, because you can't resist this. That is the truth.

GLINDA:
Well, maybe I can't. Is that so wrong? Who could?

FIYERO:
You know who could. And who has.

GLINDA:
Fiyero – I miss her too. But – we can't just stop living. No one has searched harder for her than you! But don't you see? She doesn't want to be found. You've got to face it.

FIYERO:
You're right. And look, if it'll make you happy, of course I'll marry you.

GLINDA:
But it'll make you happy too, right?

FIYERO:
Well, you know me ... I'm always happy. (He exits swiftly.)

Fiyero has called Glinda on her complicity with the Wizard. He accuses her of desiring her own power and popularity more than she desires the truth or even to help their friend. Glinda is confused by all this. She sings that her arrival at the pinnacle of achievement is "the tiniest bit unlike I anticipated." Listen to Glinda describe her doubts:

'Cause getting your dreams
It's strange, but it seems
A little – well – complicated
There's a kind of a sort of ... cost
There's a couple of things that get ... lost
There are bridges you cross
You didn't know you crossed
Until you've crossed ...

And if that joy, that thrill
Doesn't thrill like you think it will
Still ...
With this perfect finale
The cheers and the ballyhoo
Who
Wouldn't be happier?
So I couldn't be happier
Because happy is what happens
When all your dreams come true
Well, isn't it?
Happy is what happens ...
When all your dreams come true!

Like a victim, those who enjoy all the benefits of the Sacrificial System are in a unique position to see through its lies. The celebrities of our world are in a similar position and we have seen all too often how the happiness they anticipated never arrives. Instead they feel empty and unloved, even as their bank accounts are full and their fan base swells into the millions. Like Glinda, they believed that they could acquire happiness through accumulation of possessions: people, power, prestige. It is no wonder that so many celebrities fall victim to alcohol or drug addictions, depression and even suicide. How tragic it must be to have followed all the rules, done all the right things, achieved all there is to achieve, and still be unhappy. With no alternatives to happiness left, hopelessness and despair lurk behind every perfect smile.

Few of us face the realities of celebrity, but we all have to some degree experienced a sense of unease with the promises of Myth. When no matter how hard you play by the rules, no matter how successful you become at acquiring wealth, prestige, promotions, and truckloads of friends, you feel vaguely unhappy, you are being invited to journey out of the Mythological world. It's a journey worth taking because the twinge of unhappiness is your conscience calling you to account. All the things the Myth promises, from personal happiness to communities at peace with themselves, come with a price tag. The Myth gives us permission to sacrifice a few people and a few truths along the way, but conceals the cost in a shroud of silence. The way through that shroud is the willingness to experience our unhappiness fully rather than run away from it. The Myth is counting on our lack of courage here, that we'd rather be happy at someone else's expense than be unhappy with ourselves and face our own complicity in the suffering of others. The Myth is counting on us to be satisfied with the pretense of goodness rather than the real thing.

Glinda the Good shows us the way by facing her own sadness. She regrets the "couple of things" that have gotten lost, like her friendship with Elphaba and her belief in her own goodness. Her coveted relationship with Fiyero is anything but perfect and she knows in her heart the thing she most of all hopes isn't true, that Elphaba's life is at risk from the very powers she is now a part of. This is not how it's supposed to be and she fears that she may have crossed a bridge or two she wished she hadn't. Glinda is beginning to understand that the path to happiness can never involve using and abusing another human being and her understanding is born in sorrow.

Both Elphaba and Glinda have been forced to see things they didn't want to. Neither girl wanted to know that the Wonderful Wizard of Oz was behind the suffering of the Animals. It is a knowledge almost too difficult for them to bear, and we shall see in the remainder of Act Two how Elphaba and Glinda struggle to find a proper response. But neither of the girls can go back. They are incredibly unhappy and they have chosen not to anesthetize the feeling. They will live with it, accepting it as the rightful consequence of the choices they have made so far. Their unhappiness is the direct result of contact with the victims the Myth wants to hide. Many of us choose to remain within the Myth because of how painful the path out of it truly is. How many of us are willing to be unhappy, even for a little while? How many of us are willing to gaze into the eyes of our victims and see their suffering and unhappiness? Those of us brave enough to do it are the ones who gain the right to be called wonderful and good.

11

Moral Ambiguities

> It's people who claim that they're good, or anyway better than the rest of us, that you have to be wary of.
>
> MAGUIRE, *Wicked*

> The great masses of the people... will more easily fall victims to a great lie than to a small one.
>
> ADOLF HITLER (1889 – 1945)

> Of all tyrannies, a tyranny sincerely exercised for the good of its victims may be the most oppressive.
>
> C. S. LEWIS (1898 – 1963)

The dependence of the Myth on creating absolute and fixed categories of good and evil has devastating consequences. The next few scenes will reveal how the Myth corrupts relationships and identities until they threaten to poison and destroy the entire community. Specifically we will see Elphaba, who still believes in the methods of the

Sacrificial System, as she struggles in futility to differentiate herself from her enemies and find the acceptance she so desperately desires.

The last time we saw Elphaba, she was soaring high above our heads, announcing her determination to defeat the Wizard, free the flying monkeys, save Dr. Dillamond, and become more powerful than the Wizard himself. But she has not truly differentiated herself from the Wizard. Rather, she has made a 360-degree spin that has left her in the same place as she started. Instead of seeking to find her true self through an alliance with the Wizard, she now defines herself in opposition to him. In fact, she is more like him than before – since she now knows that the source of the violence against the Animals is the Wizard, and has adopted those methods as her own.

We know from experience that the use of violence by one side causes an escalation by the other, generating an endless series of reprisals that ultimately lead to complete annihilation. Observing this pattern, we feel the dizzying sensation of being caught in a Ferris wheel ride that is speeding up with every rotation. Similarly, we see in political discourse today that what passes for dialogue is really one accusation after another, ongoing attempts at defamation of character with the ultimate goal the complete humiliation of the other's public life. A political scientist from Nigeria, Kayode Fayemi, was quoted in the *New York Times* commenting on the political situation in his country, where instability threatens the top levels of government and violent militants seek to control oil-producing regions of the country. Mr. Fayemi says, "Six years down the line in the attempt to build democracy this is what we get: violence in the land, and a government in breach. The only thing happening is politics. It is motion without movement."[1]

Motion without movement is an excellent description of the constant churning and turmoil of the Sacrificial System. It is endlessly seeking scapegoats to keep the rest of the public in the dark about where evil is and our own complicity in a system that sanctifies the use of violence. How can one escape?

Elphaba wants to. She has told us that she is tired of trying to earn love, that it's time to "close my eyes and leap." But that's what the Myth expects – for Elphaba to keep her eyes closed to the futility of trying to achieve peace, freedom or love by adhering to the Mythological Rules. Not until the very end of the musical will Elphaba open her eyes, and conceive of a radical way to defeat the Myth. Right now, Elphaba is a warrior in the grand tradition of all Mythological stories, and she is in need of an ally.

Isolated and abandoned by Glinda, Elphaba must find a way to defeat the most powerful man in Oz. She turns to the only potential ally she can think of, her father, the powerful Governor of Munchkinland. Elphaba hopes that despite his rejection of her, he will stand beside her in her hour of need. Elphaba opens this next scene with her own interpretation of motion without movement. She has gone home and greets Nessarose with this angry and cynical remark: "Well, it seems the beautiful only get more beautiful, while the green just get greener." The scene unfolds to illustrate just how stagnant the Sacrificial System is as it damages all the human relationships it touches.

Elphaba pleads with Nessarose to take her side when Elphaba approaches their father. But Nessa has bad news for Elphaba – their father is dead. Cruelly, Nessa tells her that he died of shame when he heard that Elphaba scorned the Wizard and became a fugitive. Nessa has already aligned herself with her father's shame, and now refuses to help Elphaba, for she has become "an un-elected official" herself, the new Governor of Munchkinland. She can't harbor a fugitive without herself becoming an enemy of Oz. But there is more to her refusal than that. Nessarose is resentful that Elphaba has not used her powers to help her walk. She sings:

All of my life, I've depended on you
How do you think that feels?
All of my life I've depended on you
And this hideous chair with wheels!
Scrounging for scraps of pity to pick up
And longing to kick up
My heels ...

Here is another example of how there are always strings attached to love within the Sacrificial System. Elphaba may have truly loved her sister, but their relationship was forever poisoned by their father's favoritism. Nessa could never be sure of Elphaba's motives: Was Elphaba caring for her out of genuine love or to score points with their father? Elphaba herself could not be sure of her own motives. Because their father had, for his own selfish reasons, labeled one child deserving and the other not, all of his relationships became tainted by manipulation, greed and personal gain. They became transactions. The deeper one gets inside the Myth, the more difficult it becomes to believe in the possibility of unconditional giving. The unexpected gift of a black hat or a sparkling training wand generate not just gratitude, but also suspicion. Life is lived defensively. Like the dad who responds to a compliment from his teenage son with, "Okay, what do you want now?" we all wonder what even the most generous people want from us.

We are not surprised to learn that Nessa wants something from Elphaba, and it's a biggie – she wants to walk. Though Elphaba protests that Nessa does not understand how the power of the Grimmerie works, she begins chanting a spell from the magic book and the silver shoes given to Nessa by their father become enchanted. Nessa stands, then walks, and Elphaba expects Nessa's gratitude, maybe even love. But Nessa is not grateful. Her desire to walk was not an end in itself, but a gambit in her conquest of Boq's heart.

We find out that Boq has been a virtual prisoner of Nessa's and that she has victimized all of Munchkinland, stripping them of what little rights they had, in order to keep Boq at her side. As soon as Boq sees she can walk, he declares with a sense of relief that Nessa will not need him anymore, so he is free to pursue his futile love of Glinda. Nessa cannot release him so easily and uses the Grimmerie incorrectly to try to cast a spell forcing him to love her. She sings, "You're going to lose your heart to me, I tell you! If I have to ... magic spell you." She almost kills him, causing his heart to actually shrink and Elphaba has to do something quickly to save his life. Her spell allows him to live without a heart, since Nessa has destroyed his.

This scene of manipulations to compel or purchase love ends in a rather graphic lesson which Elphaba states quite clearly when she says to Nessa, "I've done everything I could for you. And it hasn't been enough.

I can offer an example of what happens when someone we love fails to uphold their end of the "aren't I good and wonderful" routine. My son, whom I deeply love, was eleven years old when we moved to a new neighborhood. We had been there maybe a week, when a neighbor confronted me in my driveway with this horrible report: She had witnessed my son and two of his friends jumping from our second story roof onto the garage and then down to the driveway. The look in her eyes and the tone of her voice as she reported this accused me in a way her words did not. I was a bad mother. I had left my child unattended and he had engaged in dangerous behavior, risking not only his own life, but also those of his friends. My response was immediate and visceral. Adrenaline rushed through my body, my face flushed and my stomach contracted into a ball. My son had ruined my reputation in this new neighborhood. I would henceforth be known as the bad mother – how could I ever recover?

My identity was tightly tied up with being a good mother – my children knew it instinctively. They would tell me so in words and cards, hugging and reassuring me that I was indeed a good mom. When that woman stood in my driveway with all her righteous indignation, I wanted to throttle my son. The offense seemed too large to forgive. Rather than a harmless prank, I perceived what he had done as a direct assault on my sense of identity.

For longer than I care to admit, I forgot that I loved my son, that he was only an eleven-year-old boy prone to silly stunts, and instead I saw him as a threat that had to be dealt with harshly. He had to learn that he was not a boy, but part of my sense of self, not a unique lovable being, but a foot soldier in the Suzanne-is-a-good-mother army. I am ashamed of the rage I felt, and grateful that I was able to moderate it enough so that I did not lash out and harm my child, either physically or emotionally. But the sense of violation was so real and so strong, that I fear I was capable of inflicting great harm. Loving others for who they are and not for what they do for you can be painfully hard.

And nothing ever will be." Love cannot be turned into a commodity that can be bought, sold, or acquired or it ceases to be love.

The sad outcome of living within the Sacrificial System is that people themselves become commodities to be used or abused. The Sacrificial System destroys our ability to love; it's as simple as that. When people become objects they can be acquired, traded, manipulated or ignored, but they cannot be loved. Love requires that we recognize the inherent worth of another human being as equal to our own. In our own lives it is possible that we can garner the strength to do that with a few people who are close to us, spouses or friends, parents or siblings. But what happens when they disappoint us, when they do or become something that does not serve our need to feel good about ourselves? Sadly, inside the Myth the room to love someone completely for who they are, and not what they can do for us, is as tiny as a broom closet.

Elphaba's interview with Nessarose was an unmitigated disaster. She has no choice now but to try to free the winged monkeys on her own. She sneaks into the Wizard's palace, but he discovers her before she can find a way to open the cages. Rather than have her arrested by his guards, the Wizard tries one more time to convince her to become his ally. He tells her how wonderful it is to be wonderful, and sings seductively of what she can have if she will stop resisting him. The labels of good and evil are so arbitrary within the Myth, that even an old humbug like the Wizard can be revered and worshipped. He explains:

> I never asked for this
> Or planned it in advance
> I was merely blown here
> By the winds of chance
> I never saw myself
> As a Solomon or Socrates
> I knew who I was:
> One of your dime a dozen
> Mediocrities
> Then suddenly I'm here
> Respected - worshipped even

Just because the folks in Oz
Needed someone to believe in

The Ozians *needed* him to be wonderful. They needed someone to believe in – that is, they needed someone who would tell them without any doubt who was good and who was evil. These are the lies they wanted to hear which the Wizard sings about to Elphaba. The Wizard sings about their "history," which unfortunately has more truth to it than not, for history is simply the record of the victors of various conflicts. There really is no other way to tell the difference between good and evil in war, because everyone is using the same methods and each side thinks they are the righteous ones. The victor wins the power to write the history books and decide whose perspective is told. Listen to how the Wizard explains it:

A man's called a traitor – or liberator
A rich man's a thief – or philanthropist
Is one a crusader – or ruthless invader
It's all in the label which
Is able to persist
There are precious few at ease
With moral ambiguities
So we act as though they don't exist

By telling the stories of our past in a way that conceals those of our enemies, we absolve ourselves of guilt in the use of our violence: Our enemies were so completely evil, we were morally justified in using violence to defeat them. If we did not believe this, we would feel guilty rather than joyful whenever we killed one of the enemy. It is not enough for our victims to be only a little bit wicked. The Scapegoating Mechanism won't work if the witch is simply a sad, green baby who never got enough attention from her father. It won't work if the victim is a good person who made a bad decision, a little bit like we are. This is the moral ambiguity that the Wizard is referring to – we simply can't have any of it within the Sacrificial System.

When we tell our history in this way, the scapegoats must be labeled as totally "other" so that we can expel them from our communities without feeling any guilt or moral discomfort. Our consciences are not only sound asleep, but our egos become inflated with a sense of ourselves as morally good. Elphaba's greenness is the sign for the Ozians that she is completely, unambiguously "other," and therefore, totally evil. It is a sad truth of the Sacrificial System that differences are dangerous. They put one at risk for being a scapegoat and, therefore, a victim of violence.

This is the origin of the rampant political correctness in our culture. On the plus side, political correctness is an attempt to live outside the Myth. Trying to be sensitive to the sensitivity of others, we do our absolute best to glorify differences rather than demonize them. It is a noble effort. We are aware of the truth the Myth wants to hide from us, that scapegoating victims are in fact completely innocent of the accusations against them. So we tiptoe around differences to avoid scapegoating anyone – especially those who claim to be scapegoats. We are very careful with our language because no one wants to be a victimizer. But no matter how careful we are, it seems that there is no way to avoid giving offense – the insult and anger that often greets our most tentative efforts at giving honor instead of shame often leave us gasping for air and feeling a bit like victims ourselves.

What is going on here? The phenomenon of political correctness reveals another trap for victims within the Sacrificial System. As if being silenced, exiled or lynched weren't bad enough, there are psychological risks as well. The first trap we talked about in Chapter 8 is that victims of oppression, like the stereotypical angry feminist, are locked in combat with their oppressors to not only halt the oppression but to cure the damage done to them. Victims often spend their lives trying to acquire from their victimizers the love and affirmation that was withheld from them. It's as if they cannot believe in their own lovability unless their oppressor believes it first. From deep within the Myth, they believe that love can be coerced or acquired if they only demand it loudly enough.

The second trap is what gives rise to that uncomfortable feeling you get when you are trying to practice political correctness and the whole thing backfires. The problem is that the ones who are claiming victim status for themselves believe completely in themselves as victims. Within the Myth people are either good or evil, victims or victimizers. So if they are victims, they believe there is no way they can ever be victimizers. They are at risk for a different sort of blindness – they can clearly see that victims (themselves) are innocent but they can never see the ways in which they themselves can become victimizers. In the arena of political correctness, self-proclaimed victims hold individuals and the entire society hostage to their demands and they are never able to conceive of the ways in which they are themselves repeating the oppression. Deluded about the universality of their innocence, they can become self-righteousness and militant in their crusading for justice. Structural innocence in one particular circumstance becomes the basis for their identity. They become "victimary" thinkers, always victims, always innocent, always good.

René Girard remarked during a panel presentation at a conference in Ottawa in 2006, that when people profess to understand scapegoating, they offer as proof the evidence of their own victimization. This is the trap of political correctness. René dismissed such comments, saying, "The story of the victim is everyone's story!"[2] Instead, he wanted a story recognizing one's own complicity as a perpetrator. This is the more difficult story to tell. Admitting to one's role as a victimizer requires a courage few of us possess. Everyone, it seems, will confess to being a victim, but no one wants to admit to being an oppressor.

Elphaba's longing for love and acceptance has so bound her into a victim identity that she needs to believe she can get from the Wizard what he promises. For a moment she is seduced by the Wizard's song, so she makes a bargain with the Wizard, a transaction for her allegiance. She demands that he release the Monkeys. The Wizard agrees, but Elphaba discovers Dr. Dillamond hidden beneath a dark shroud. He is being held prisoner and has lost his power of speech. Seeing Dr. Dillamond's plight and hearing the plaintive sound of his muffled voice, Elphaba is horrified by how easily the Wizard seduced her. She sees that she has come dangerously close to becoming exactly like her enemy and she shouts at the Wizard, "Do you know my heart's desire? It's to fight you 'till the day I die!" But how do you fight evil within the Myth without becoming evil yourself? The means become the end; your methods become the outcome. The only way for Elphaba to become truly different from the Wizard and free of her victim identity is to find another way to fight him. If she uses his methods of violence and coercion, if she hates him as much as he hates the Animals, if she is willing to use any means to destroy him, she will be just like him once again.

When Elphaba declares her opposition to the Wizard, he fears for his life and summons his guards, climbing back into the giant Head – inside the Myth – as if he can hide from her there. One of the guards is Fiyero. Glinda enters too, having heard the commotion, and is at first happy to see that Elphaba is alive and unharmed. But she is taken aback when Fiyero appears to oppose the Wizard and side with Elphaba. Indeed, he declares his intention to run away with her and Glinda is overcome with a sense of betrayal. The Wizard offers to soothe her pain with a swig from a green bottle, which she refuses. In spite of any insights Glinda may have achieved so far, she becomes blinded by her rage toward Elphaba, who is now her rival for Fiyero's affection. Remember that Glinda promised to help Elphaba become popular as long as Glinda was more popular! Now Elphaba has surpassed her teacher and become the kind of girl that Fiyero can love.

Can Glinda find it in herself to be happy for her friend? Does she have the courage that love can give her? Not yet, for Glinda discards her friendship with Elphaba, forgetting how sad she was that she had sacrificed it for Fiyero's love. Caught up in conflict with Elphaba, she sacrifices their friendship all over again by giving Morrible and the Wizard the key to defeating her friend. "Use her sister," Glinda tells them. "Spread a rumor. Make her think her sister is in trouble and she will fly to her side ... and you'll have her." Dear Glinda, who wants nothing more than to be good, commits the wickedest deed in the entire show.

12

The Road of Good Intentions

With mere good intentions, hell is proverbially paved.

WILLIAM JAMES, US Pragmatist philosopher & psychologist (1842 – 1910)

Men are only clever at shifting blame from their own shoulders to those of others.

TITUS LIVIUS, Roman author & historian (59 BC – 17 AD)

At this point in the show, the audience has come to love both Glinda and Elphaba. No longer locked into roles of Good Witch and Bad Witch for us or for themselves, they are two good people trying to do their best in a rather horrible situation. Though we know that deep inside both girls want to do the right thing, the choices they make hurt themselves and others because no other outcome is possible within the Myth. The Myth says that violence can be good and other human beings can be used and abused to satisfy one's wants and desires. The *Wicked* Truth, however, is that there is another way to be a good person, one that will bring bad deeds out into the open rather than conceal them. This way to morality recognizes the impossibility of Good Violence and demands the courage of the de-Mythologizing spirit that wants more than the pretense of goodness. This other way flips the Sacrificial Formula on its head – instead of willingly allowing another to suffer for my own good, I will choose to endure suffering for the good of others. The next few scenes illustrate how difficult yet how powerfully transformative such a decision can be.

Glinda's betrayal of Elphaba will lead to devastating loss of life, yet she seems unaware of how terrible a deed she has committed. Morrible and the Wizard know how formidable an enemy Elphaba has become. They did everything they could to convince her to join forces with them because they, of all the people in Oz, understand how powerful she is. But instead, they failed in the worst way by strengthening Elphaba's determination to defeat their plans to destroy the Animals and maintain their hold on power. Glinda's suggestion that they spread a rumor that Nessarose is in danger doesn't seem bold enough. What's needed is a sure-fire plan to defeat Elphaba and rumors won't do it. Morrible offers to create a real threat to Nessa's life, a destructive change in the weather, and the Wizard agrees.

Are Morrible and the Wizard two wicked people doing wicked things? We don't know enough about Morrible to answer that question, but we have seen the Wizard's heart. He has told us he considers himself unworthy of the title Wonderful and that he desires to give the people of Oz the powerful and benevolent leader they seem to need. As I said before, I take the Wizard at his word not because I know he is a truth-teller, but because I know such a situation can happen within the Myth. He believes with all his heart that he is good and so feels no guilt about his methods. I think it's fair to say that the Wizard, Elphaba and Glinda are all good people caught in the Myth's tangle of lies.

Within the Myth, enemies on both sides of a conflict can claim the mantle of goodness and so good and evil begin to seem like relative terms. It all seems to be a matter of perspective and produces such bizarre parallels as President Bush calling Iraq part of the Axis of evil[1] and Saddam Hussein telling his people that by opposing the United States they are "fight[ing] evil in the world."[2] Or candidates in a political campaign calling each other liars or cheats or traitors. The accusations are true from the relative perspective of the one making the accusation. However, these accusations are not about truth. They are part of the smokescreen that conceals truth and hides innocence so that the Sacrificial Mechanism can function. They are not intended to be reasonable arguments for or against any opinion or position. Instead, name-calling and accusations are offered as undeniable justifications for hatred and demonization – the precursors to the use of violence.

After Morrible and the Wizard plot Nessarose's destruction, Glinda walks mournfully across the stage singing of her broken heart. She mirrors Elphaba's lyrics, "There's a girl I know/ He loves her so/ I'm not that girl." Glinda is completely blind to the joy that Elphaba and Fiyero share. She cannot imagine that their love has nothing to do with her. All she can imagine is that they have deliberately set out to wound and betray her, and so she does the same thing to them. Endless reprisals, motion without movement. Good Violence committed without remorse.

Fiyero and Elphaba love each other in a way that does not exist within the Myth. He sings of "seeing through different eyes" and we realize that he has rejected the definition of goodness and evil offered by the Myth, which measures the worth of a person by what they can do for you. Associating with angry, green, outcast Elphaba does no one any good, particularly now that she is the declared enemy of the Wizard. But Fiyero is no longer blinded by the Myth. He sees Elphaba for who she truly is, and offers her the love and acceptance she hoped she would get from the Wizard. Remember her song in Act One, "The Wizard and I"? She explained what she hoped would happen when she met the Wizard:

> ... With all his wizard wisdom
> By my looks, he won't be blinded
> Do you think the Wizard is dumb?
> Or like Munchkins, so small-minded?
> No! He'll say to me:
> "I see who you truly are,
> A girl on whom I can rely!"
> And that's how we'll begin
> The Wizard and I ...

Ironically, the Wizard *did* see who Elphaba truly was, but his reaction was to completely reject her and seek her destruction – not the outcome Elphaba was hoping for. Rather than offer to de-greenify her, the Wizard plotted her death. Within the Myth, it's not okay to be who you truly are if it conflicts with the desires of the most powerful. The Myth demands compliance, even from the green-skinned outcast, and when it doesn't get what it wants it reacts with terrifying rage. In the 1939 movie, when the four friends first meet the Wizard, he thunders and erupts like a volcano and they tremble in fear. That howling, smoking head of the movie is the perfect image of the greeting you will receive from the Myth if you dare to question it in any way.

Fiyero reacts completely differently than the Wizard. When he sees Elphaba for what she truly is, he loves her. Rather than offer to de-greenify her, this is what he tells her:

ELPHABA:
I just wish ...

FIYERO:
What?

ELPHABA:
I wish I could be beautiful ... for you.

FIYERO:
Elphaba ...

ELPHABA:
Don't tell me that I am, you don't need to lie to me.

FIYERO:
It's not lying! It's ... uh ... it's looking at things another way.

What is this other way of looking at things? It is the path to true goodness, for it refuses to turn people into objects that can be bartered for peace or popularity or power. Fiyero now dwells in a land where no one has to pay for love. It is freely given and freely received. While the Wizard's reaction to Elphaba represents the Myth, Fiyero's reaction represents Unconditional Love. It is the love that transformed hatred into friendship for Elphaba and Glinda in Act One. Even when Galinda only pretended to offer something for nothing – the black hat – it had the power to create new and powerful bonds of friendship and respect.

Because Elphaba finds a way to accept Fiyero's love for her, she believes for the first time in her life in her own lovability. This frees her from her victim identity. She no longer needs anything from the Wizard – whether or not he ever understands how truly wonderful she is matters only to him now. Now she is free to imagine a new way out of her problems in Oz. But she is about to suffer a terrible loss, a wound inflicted from her dearest friend that threatens everything she has gained so far.

Nessarose is killed by a falling house caught up in the cyclone conjured by Morrible. Rather than the gleeful celebration that greets this death in the 1939 movie, the audience in the theater reacts with sadness. We have seen the reason why Nessa became so wicked and we grieve for her. No longer a fairy tale character, this wicked witch is too human for us to feel happy that she is dead. Like many of us, she longed for a love she couldn't have; she believed in a father's love that was not love at all; she felt abandoned by her sister and victimized by physical limitations. One of my favorite expressions is "there but for the grace of God go I," and I feel that applies to Nessarose – I could easily have made the same choices as she along the way from innocent schoolgirl to possessive, jealous lover. This time I can't be glad she's dead. For once, I am moved to mourn the wicked.

How will Elphaba react to her sister's death? She meets Glinda at the site and as they talk she realizes that Glinda was behind this, however unwittingly. Elphaba berates Glinda for not thinking, for not realizing what Morrible would do with her suggestion to get to Elphaba through her sister. Their anger escalates into cruel taunts over who is more worthy of Fiyero's love and soon the girls actually come to blows, striking each other in anger, their friendship utterly forgotten.

BLESSED ARE THOSE WHO MOURN

The phrase "blessed are those who mourn, for they will be comforted," found in Matthew 5:44 of the Christian gospels takes on a new meaning when examined outside the Myth. As part of The Beatitudes of Jesus, a collection of sayings about how to be blessed and find happiness, this saying seems to be paradoxical. "Blessed" can be translated into "happy," as in "happy are those who mourn." How can grieving people be happy? The assurance of comfort does offer some happiness in the midst of grief, but it may be that comfort is not offered in response to the suffering caused by grief. Perhaps it is offered to cause us to mourn. By that I mean, those who choose to mourn rather than celebrate a death are taking a courageous step outside of the world of Myth.

Imagine if you were the only one in Munchkinland who felt a twinge of regret at Nessa's death. Now imagine what it might feel like if you were at the celebration and dared to say, "Um, excuse me? Should we really be singing like this? I mean, 'ding-dong the witch is dead' is sort of cruel, isn't it? What about her family and friends? Aren't they upset that she's gone?" At the very least, you would be accused of being a party-pooper, maybe naïve and sentimental, and at worse you would risk becoming a victim of violence yourself. You would certainly be ruining the happiness that everyone is feeling by your refusal to join in the celebration.

But as the saying goes, happy are those who mourn, not happy are those who celebrate. This saying reverses the typical order found within the Sacrificial System and insists that true happiness is found when we dare to mourn the death of even the wickedest witch. By offering us comfort in advance, this saying encourages us to take the risk that accompanies such grief within the Sacrificial System.

Quickly, however, their petty fight is put into terrifying perspective when the Wizard's guards arrive and not far behind them is Fiyero. When the guards attempt to arrest Elphaba, Fiyero threatens to harm Glinda unless they release her. It is a foolish act, for as soon as Elphaba flees, the guards take him away to torture him until he confesses to Elphaba's whereabouts. Both Glinda and Elphaba are devastated by this unintended consequence of their rivalry. He whom they both professed to love is the one whose very life is now at risk.

With Fiyero captured, maybe already dead, Elphaba wonders how it is that things ended up so terribly. Her desperation leads her to assess her past actions with "an ice cold eye." No guilt or shame that she might feel over such a frank appraisal of her life could compare to the depth of despair she feels over Fiyero's fate. So she does what most people trapped within the Myth never do, she asks a question the Myth tries to suppress: What is goodness? As Elphaba sings in "No Good Deed":

> One question haunts and hurts
> Too much, too much to mention:
> Was I really seeking good
> Or just seeking attention?
> Is that all good deeds are
> When looked at with an ice-cold eye?
> If that's all good deeds are
> Maybe that's the reason why ...
>
> No good deed goes unpunished
> All helpful urges should be circumvented
> No good deed goes unpunished
> Sure, I meant well –
> Well, look at what well-meant did ...

Elphaba feels that no matter how hard she has tried to do good, it has always backfired. Her attempt to win her father's affection by taking care of Nessarose got her nowhere with him. Her attempt to win Nessarose's love by miraculously healing her crippled legs failed to soften Nessa's heart.

Trying to help Dr. Dillamond has done him no good at all and only turned Elphaba into an enemy of the Wizard. Worst of all, accepting Fiyero's love has led to his imprisonment and torture, maybe even his death.

Why have all her attempted good deeds gone bad? Maybe, she wonders, it's because her motives were all wrong. Maybe she was thinking more about herself and her need for approval than about the needs of the ones she wanted to help. If good deeds are not good deeds at all, but merely attempts to earn love, then no wonder "no good deed goes unpunished." As she learned from her failed attempt to earn Nessarose's love, that which must be earned is not love at all.

She sings, "Sure I meant well, but look what well meant did." All she can see is the wrong she has done and the hurt she has caused to the people she loved. She sings:

All right, enough – so be it!
So be it then:
Let all Oz be agreed
I'm Wicked through and through
Since I cannot succeed
Fiyero, saving you
I promise no good deed
Will I attempt to do
Again
Ever again
No good deed
Will I do
Again!

Elphaba is learning that her attempts at love were not love at all. Because of Fiyero, she is learning what true love is. Love is not love if a win/loss calculation is involved. Perhaps one day we might be lucky enough to have someone respond to a Mythological "good deed" of ours as if it were truly good, as Elphaba did for Glinda. Elphaba now wears the black hat as an outward sign of her friendship with Glinda, that once she was loved completely, freely. To practice this kind of love we must be willing to endure rather than cause suffering, even if we must endure the suffering of admitting that we weren't good at all.

Wicked wants us to be brave enough to face the possibility that because we have needed so desperately to be good, we may have too willingly sacrificed an innocent person to our noble goals. Because we believed so much in the goodness and truth of our goals, perhaps we compromised those goals by using methods that we condemn as cruel and inhuman when used by our enemies. Good people do bad things when their need to *be* good becomes more important than their need to *do* good.

It is important to understand that the true hero of any de-Mythologizing story like *Wicked* is not the one who succeeds at any cost, who out-powers the powerful, but the one who is willing to admit to his own mistakes. The de-Mythologizing spirit gives us the strength to let go of our need to think of ourselves as good, at least as it is defined by the Myth. Succeeding within the Myth demands the courage of the warrior. To destroy the Myth, one must have the courage of love.

Does Elphaba have this kind of courage? When describing the way the world views the scapegoat, Girard referenced Psalm 31:11-13.[3] The psalms predominantly represent the voice of a victim of persecution crying out in anguish and anger. Listen to the voice of the psalmist: "I am contemptible, loathsome to my neighbors, to my friends a thing of fear ..." When Elphaba sings, "I'm wicked through and through," she tells us that she believes herself to be contemptible, loathsome, a thing of fear. Elphaba is still trapped by the world's definition of her as evil. She can't seem to find a way out, so she surrenders to it completely.

13

For Good

Evil is always possible. Goodness is a difficulty.

ANNE RICE, US novelist (1941 –)

One never learns how the witch became wicked, or whether that was the right choice for her – is it ever the right choice? Does the devil ever struggle to be good again, or if so is he not a devil?

MAGUIRE, *Wicked*

Aim above morality. Be not simply good, be good for something.

HENRY DAVID THOREAU,
US Transcendentalist author (1817 – 1862)

Elphaba has succumbed to one of the dangers of waking up from the Myth. She is giving in to despair. She has been confronted with the harsh reality of exactly what passes for goodness within the Sacrificial System. Either it is an entire sham, like the Wizard's wonderfulness, or it is a dismal failure, like all her good deeds. She is beginning to suspect that goodness is not possible at all.

Evil, on the other hand, appears to be everywhere. Not only are the Wizard and Morrible inflicting death and destruction on anyone who opposes them, but also good people are committing evil deeds without remorse, like the fearful Ozians who believe Elphaba is a wicked witch. In the next scene, we find ourselves once again in the midst of the angry mob that has been stirred up against our heroine. These are the same Ozians we met at the opening of the show, the ones who needed to believe they were good and so they looked for evil somewhere outside of themselves. In the same way that we saw Elphaba trapped into defining herself as "other than the Wizard," the Ozians know they are good because they are "not the Wicked Witch." Listen to what they say:

OZIANS:
Go and hunt her
And find her
And kill her

VICIOUS WOMAN:
Good fortune, witch hunters!

OZIANS:
Go and hunt her
And find her
And kill her

RABID MAN:
Kill the witch!

OZIANS:
Wickedness must be punished
Evil effectively e-liminated
Wickedness must be punished
Kill the witch!

The open bloodlust of the mob is possible because they have totally demonized Elphaba. She is one hundred percent wicked and they are one hundred percent good. This means that she is no longer an Ozian like they are, but something so totally other that killing her would not be a crime but a virtue. When killing becomes virtuous and remorseless, we are less likely to ask ourselves if we harbor un-virtuous motives. We are less likely to wonder if we have found a truly wicked witch or are persecuting an innocent girl. It is no wonder that Elphaba gives in to despair – when good people seem unable to combat evil without committing evil deeds themselves, there is little reason to hope.

Is there anything that can open the Ozians' eyes to Elphaba's innocence? Will they ever learn to recognize the difference between an innocent victim and the real threat to the peace of Oz that is the Wizard? To know the answers we must truly ask the same questions of our own world, and not merely as an intellectual exercise. There are real threats to our safety and security, and we would do well to identify them with some measure of certainty. I, for one, am not interested in wasting time and money chasing after a lonely green girl while a truly Wicked Witch is busy plotting my demise, gleefully cackling over my misdirection. If, as I suggested earlier, the musical is suggesting that evil does exist but we have been looking for it in all the wrong places, where are the right places?

During our journey through the Land of Oz with Elphaba and Glinda, we have learned two things about where evil can be found. We have become aware that everyone of us is capable of evil deeds, even when we are trying our hardest to be good. Evil is not a quality of being that is fixed and unchangeable like a genetic trait. Exactly what activates the capacity for evil is the second thing we have learned on our journey: a belief in Good Violence. When any one of us falls under the spell of the Myth about good and evil, we become the gods of our own kingdoms. Our wants and desires, even our lives, become more valuable than anyone else's and thus any action we take on our own behalf is totally justified and morally right. We can use and abuse others, and their suffering and defeat becomes a cause of celebration. We have learned that evil deeds are possible when good people become blind followers of the

Mythological Rules. The search for evil begins inside us and extends into every region where Myth reigns unchallenged.

The Ozian crowd has been our example of blind adherence to the Rules. In their eagerness to think of themselves as good, they have believed the accusations of evil made against Elphaba and the truth is, they actually do feel good about themselves as they engage in their search-and-destroy mission. Myth, as we know, contains a little bit of truth. But there is also a lie: that what passes for goodness isn't good at all. In the next scene, insincerity is confronted head on as Morrible cynically challenges Glinda's newfound concern for victims. Glinda is upset about the false accusations Morrible is making about Elphaba and she is worried for her friend's life and for Fiyero's fate. When she confronts Morrible, this terrible spin-doctor to the Wizard calls her on the bargain Glinda has herself made:

> MORRIBLE:
> Now, you listen to me, Missy. The rest of Oz may have fallen for that "aren't I good" routine, but I know better. You've wanted this from the beginning ... and now you're getting what you wanted. So just smile and wave and shut up! Good fortune, good fortune, witches hunters!

Ah, Madame Morrible – she knows better than anyone that the type of goodness you can achieve within the Myth is nothing but a sham. Deeply enslaved to the Myth, Morrible is the worst sort of person because she knows the costs and yet still she does not care. Her mistake is to think that Glinda is just like her. Naïve Glinda has made the bargain the Myth demands: To be good she willingly paid the price, crossed a few bridges without thinking or caring who was being sacrificed to achieve her ends. But the difference between Glinda and Morrible is the degree of courage each possesses to face the suffering of her victims and admit her own mistakes.

The arrest of Dr. Dillamond, the suffering of the monkeys, the death of Nessarose and Elphaba's grief – none of that affects Morrible because her need to be right is stronger than her need to be truly good. She is not brave enough to take in the evidence of suffering her actions cause and admit that she was wrong, so she will never change. Glinda, on the other hand, is one of the most courageous fictional characters I have met. As we have discovered, Glinda is willing to be wrong and to suffer the unhappiness that admission will cause. Her willingness to endure unhappiness and personal suffering for the sake of others is the spark required for her to change.

But within the Myth, change is not an option. People are all good or all bad, all the time. The first two Mythological Rules say it well:

MYTHOLOGICAL RULE #1
Evil can and must be identified with absolute certainty.

MYTHOLOGICAL RULE #2
We are good because we hate evil.

But the *Wicked* Truths revealed by the musical proclaim a different story:

Wicked TRUTH #1
Everyone is capable of being both good and evil.

Wicked TRUTH #2
Evil hides by accusing innocent others of being evil.

Because of the hard and fast categories of good and evil that exist within Myth, there is very little room for good people to do bad things or for bad people to regret their actions and reform their lives. Outside the Myth, however, the possibility always exists for error and recovery, mistakes and correction. You may be familiar with the biblical language for this very human reality: sin and repentance. Sin means nothing more than error, like an arrow shot that misses the bull's eye. Repentance means to turn away from the error to face in a new direction. The language of sin and repentance is language that can only be spoken with integrity outside the Myth. Outside the Myth, we recognize our kinship with all human beings: We are all sinners standing in need of forgiveness. Instead of fast categories of good and evil, we live within the permanence of change. Glinda has come to recognize that being good means admitting to the possibility of your own faults.

The difference between good and evil within and outside the Myth is a little like the difference between a still photograph and a motion picture. Within the Myth, goodness and evil are as fixed as the dated haircut in your high school graduation picture. Outside the Myth, each of us exists not in a still photo from a yearbook, but in a moving picture. We are living, changing people on a journey that includes love scenes and conflict, tranquil panoramic vistas and painful close-ups that show our every wart, wrinkle and flaw. Deciding whether someone is good or evil from one publicity photo taken from that motion picture is very Mythological. Thank goodness none of us is judged by our high school haircuts. Hairstyles change and so do we.

Because of the ever-present possibility for change that exists outside the Myth, the death and destruction of even the most wicked person is not a cause for celebration. Why? Because the only thing that can utterly eliminate the possibility for transformation is death. Killing an enemy is like a scene from a motion picture that is chronicling two lives, our enemy's and ours. For a while our stories take place in separate plot lines, but at the moment of confrontation our paths cross and from then on only one of us lives to star in the rest of the movie. When one begins to dwell outside the Myth, killing an enemy is not a success but a failure. As we stand over the grave of our enemy we wonder if, rather than having destroyed wickedness, we have destroyed this man or woman's chances to change. Might this be the grave of a Glinda or Fiyero from the opening scene of the musical?

Before we take the ultimate act of depriving someone of their lives, we must also be sure that we are not caught up like the Ozian mob in pursuing a victim of false accusations. We can become so caught up in false witch hunts, that we never discover the man behind the curtain. Perhaps we are content for him to remain hidden from view because the Sacrificial System, however flawed we now see it to be, does successfully provide a way for us to discharge our pent-up anger and resentments. Our violence is directed outward rather than at each other and so we succeed in preventing our own destruction. We have clung to the Sacrificial System for so long because it preserves the balance in our community. Leaving behind the only way we know how to achieve peace, however false or temporary it may be, is a frightening prospect.

But *Wicked* has been gently coaxing us to imagine another way to feel good about ourselves and to achieve a true and lasting peace. As we near the final curtain of this marvelous musical, we can now recognize and name the ways in which the Myth operates in our lives and communities. *Wicked* has given us a way to talk about the unease we feel and the unhappiness that haunts us when all our dreams come true. And it has provided a way for us to hear the cries of the victims of the Sacrificial System. And now, through the struggles of Elphaba and Glinda to be truly good people and truly good friends, we will witness an end to their story that offers a way for us to begin living outside the Myth.

The musical is nearing its finale at the moment of greatest danger to both girls. Elphaba is hiding from the Witch Hunters with Chistery and the other flying monkeys in a distant abandoned castle that belongs to Fiyero's family. Glinda has arrived just ahead of the mob to warn Elphaba, but Elphaba is more concerned about Glinda's safety than her own. Listen to the parting words of two good friends:

> ELPHABA:
> You can't be found here! You must go.
>
> GLINDA:
> No.
>
> ELPHABA:
> You must – please.
>
> GLINDA:
> Then I'll go and tell them. I'll tell everyone the truth.
>
> ELPHABA:
> No! They'll only turn against you.

GLINDA:
I don't care!

ELPHABA:
Well, I do! Promise me, you won't try to clear my name ... promise.

GLINDA:
Elphie, no I—

ELPHABA:
Promise.

GLINDA:
I promise. But I don't understand.

Elphaba insists that Glinda not try to "clear her name." Why? You'd think she would want her story to be told, even if it was too late to do her any good. At least after the mob had destroyed her, they might have some measure of regret for what they had done. But Elphaba knows how dangerous it is to be associated with someone whom the crowd believes is irredeemable. As surely as they are one hundred percent good, so is Elphaba one hundred percent evil. Through association, they would inevitably come to believe the same about Glinda.

Though Glinda promises not to say a word, we know that she has not kept that promise. The entire musical has been Glinda's story of how her friend, Elphaba, was wrongly accused by the Wizard. It seems that she was willing to risk her life for the truth after all. Perhaps Glinda is worthy of the trust Elphaba now places in her. Listen:

ELPHABA:
I'm limited
Just look at me – I'm limited
And just look at you –
You can do all I couldn't do, Glinda

ELPHABA:
(Spoken) *Here. Go on. Take it.* (Hands Her The Grimmerie.)

GLINDA:
(Spoken) *Elphie ... you know I can't read this ... Elphie ...*

ELPHABA:
(Spoken) *Well then, you'll have to learn*
(Sung) Because now it's up to you
For both of us - Now it's up to you ...

ELPHABA:
You're the only friend I've ever had.

GLINDA:
And I've had so many friends ... but only one – that mattered.

Elphaba claims to be limited, which is actually a good thing. She has finally realized that the only way to be truly different from the Wizard is to reject his wicked methods, such as scapegoating and the heartless use of violence. The irony is that by accepting limits, for the first time in her life, Elphaba is truly free to be herself and make her own decisions.

Within the Myth, freedom is the rallying cry, but what it usually means is "my freedom at the expense of yours." Outside the Myth, there is much that limits our actions. Freedom is not possible without accepting the responsibilities of one's actions. There is no "my freedom" or "your freedom," there is only "our freedom." If my freedom must be bought with yours, then it's not real freedom, but an exchange made within the Sacrificial System. The same can be said for peace. Peace is not possible if it is only peace for some and not all, as it is in Oz. If the citizens of the Emerald City enjoy peace, but the Animals do not, that is Mythological peace, a poor and pale imitation of the real thing. True peace is always universal.

Yes, there is much that limits us when we dwell outside the Myth. But it is those limits that lead to true happiness. Glinda has been our guide in this area, showing how the promise of happiness within the Myth is a false one. By being honest about her unhappiness she revealed how the methods of the Creed of Self-Worship will inevitably backfire. Glinda will no longer use or abuse anyone to get what she wants because she now knows that's not the way to true happiness. Wiser, aware of her own failings, and bearing the burden of her mistakes, Glinda may turn out to be a much better leader than the Wizard ever was. For Oz's sake, we hope so.

In the face of threats from our enemies, our new awareness offers many reasons to proceed with caution, but caution has its risks. Sometimes accepting limits on our behavior is risky business. The longer we wait to respond to a perceived threat to our lives, the more our own lives are in danger. If we hesitate to destroy our enemy when we have the opportunity, it may mean that it is we who will be killed and our enemy who will star in the end of the motion picture. Is that a risk worth taking? Perhaps we might be willing to accept the risk for ourselves, but what about people in our care, defenseless or innocent people who will die if we don't destroy the threat first? These are terrible choices that face our political and military leaders and we are the innocent ones whose lives they are duty-bound to protect.

There is nothing about life outside the Myth that suggests it is good and right to let innocent people die and wicked people triumph. On the contrary, the non-Mythological worldview is so attuned to the suffering of innocent people that there is a moral imperative within it to protect and defend the innocent and end all suffering where we can. Mahatma Gandhi's son once raised this very issue with his father, the 20th century's most famous practitioner of non-violence. Referring to a time when Gandhi was beaten up by some Indians in South Africa his son asked him: "'How could I have protected you nonviolently, if I was with you?' In reply, Gandhi said, 'If necessary to protect someone you love, some violence may be used but only enough to protect the threatened person.' Yet, again, on another occasion he said no violence should be done to anyone in a political campaign. 'I am prepared to die, but never kill for a cause.'"[1]

This is an important distinction. When we decide that it is time to use violence to protect an innocent person, we are actually putting our lives and our goodness at risk. We are saying, in effect, "I will risk using violence for your sake. I will accept that I may die defending you. I will also accept the responsibility for taking another person's life for your sake." Once outside the Myth, we become acutely aware that violence is never good and that people cannot use violence as a way to achieve goodness. This is why Gandhi said he would be prepared to die for a cause, but not kill for it. Living outside the Myth requires that our methods be as just and noble and good as our ends.

But Myth gives us a bye on our methods. Here again are Rules #3 and #4:

MYTHOLOGICAL RULE #3
There is Good Violence and Bad Violence. Good Violence is when good people kill bad people. Bad Violence is when bad people kill good people.

MYTHOLOGICAL RULE #4
The Sacrificial Formula: Someone can be sacrificed for my good or the good of my community. The end justifies the means.

Within the Myth, if our ends are good enough, then our violence is good, too. Outside the Myth, however, that is simply not the case. Here are the *Wicked* Truths we have learned from the musical:

Wicked TRUTH #3
There is no Good Violence or Bad Violence; there is only violence.

Wicked TRUTH #4
The means become the end.

Elphaba has been our guide, teaching us that if we adopt the methods of violence then our goals become corrupted. When violence is our method of choice, we become identical to our enemies: two combatants who will destroy and kill for an ideology.

Because of the limits we accept outside the Myth, we work our hardest to avoid using violence. We cannot think of ourselves as good if we have used violence to achieve our ends. In religious language, we would say that every act of violence is something for which we must repent and ask forgiveness. It is a burden some heroic people assume on our behalf, willingly risking their own goodness to protect us from violence. I am speaking of statesmen, the police and the military, men and women who know too well how destructive the methods of violence are to those who employ them. Soldiers and police officers shun honors and modestly refuse our praise because they know in their hearts that goodness has failed when a gun is fired. I grieve every day for the toll that violence and war places on these heroes, the loss of life they suffer as well as the weight of moral responsibility the survivors bear throughout their lives. Paul Rieckhoff, a former infantry officer and author of the book *Chasing Ghosts* puts it this way:

> Asking someone to die for their country might not be the biggest thing you can ask ... Asking my guys to kill, on my orders – as an officer, that's difficult. I'm telling that kid to squeeze that round off and take a man's life. And then he's got that baggage for the rest of his life. That's what you have to live with.[2]

In a review of the World War II movie, *Flags of our Fathers*, directed by Clint Eastwood, Manohla Dargis wrote:

> What do we want from war films? Entertainment, mostly, a few hours' escape to other lands and times, as well as something excitingly different, something reassuringly familiar. If *Flags of our Fathers* feels so unlike most war movies and sounds so contrary to the usual political rhetoric, it is not because it affirms that war is hell, which it does with unblinking, graphic brutality. It's because Mr. Eastwood insists, with a moral certitude that is all too rare in our movies, that we extract an unspeakable cost when we ask men to kill other men. There is never any doubt in the film that the country needed to fight this war, that it was necessary; it is the horror at such necessity that defines *Flags of Our Fathers*, not exultation.[3]

We do not honor such sacrifices enough. Perhaps we are unable. But the most meaningful honor we can bestow on the men and women

UNITED STATES
INSTITUTE OF PEACE

Everyone knows about the Department of Defense, but did you know that our government funds an institute dedicated to the study and promotion of peace? It's called the United States Institute of Peace (USIP) and here is its mission statement:

> The United States Institute of Peace is an independent, nonpartisan, national institution established and funded by Congress. Its goals are to help prevent and resolve violent international conflicts, promote post-conflict stability and democratic transformations, and increase peacebuilding capacity, tools, and intellectual capital worldwide. The Institute does this by empowering others with knowledge, skills, and resources, as well as by its direct involvement in peacebuilding efforts around the globe.*

The USIP provides support in theaters of conflict such as Afghanistan, the Balkans, Iraq, Sudan and Nigeria by offering programs to facilitate dialogue between the warring parties, provide leadership training and workshops in conflict management as well as programs that promote the rule of law and the building of civil society institutions. It conducts and publishes reports on all aspects of peacemaking, conflict resolution and community building and I bet you've never heard of it.

Although the framers of the constitution debated setting up a department dedicated to international peace on an equal footing with the War Department**, the USIP was not funded by Congress until 1984. The projected 2007 budget is almost $27 million dollars***. Not an insignificant amount of money, but it pales in comparison to the $419 billion spent by the Department of Defense in 2006****. For every $100 spent by the USIP, the Department of Defense spends $1.5 million.

...continued on next page

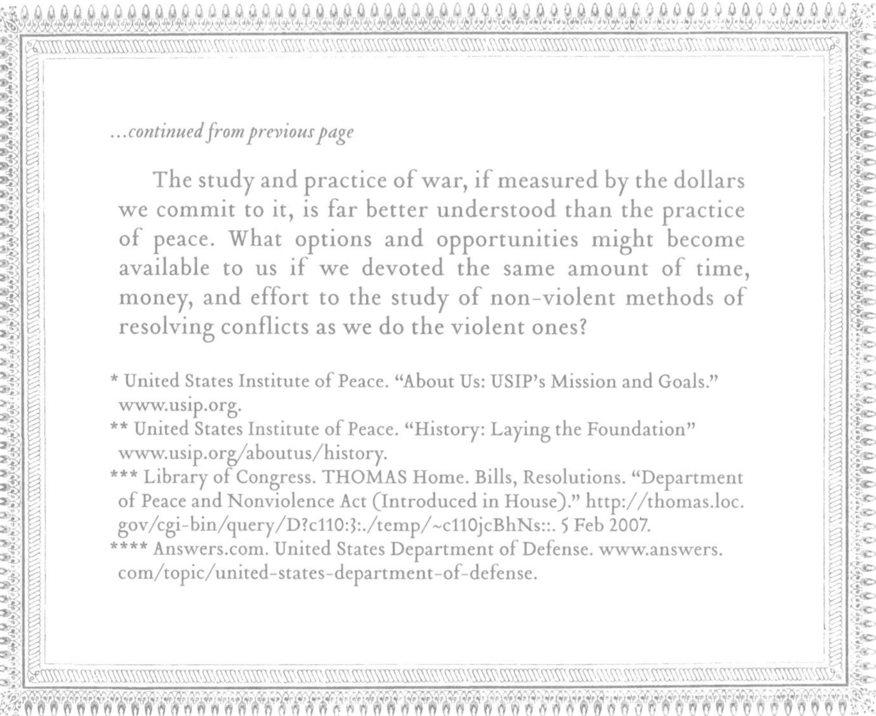
...continued from previous page

The study and practice of war, if measured by the dollars we commit to it, is far better understood than the practice of peace. What options and opportunities might become available to us if we devoted the same amount of time, money, and effort to the study of non-violent methods of resolving conflicts as we do the violent ones?

* United States Institute of Peace. "About Us: USIP's Mission and Goals." www.usip.org.
** United States Institute of Peace. "History: Laying the Foundation" www.usip.org/aboutus/history.
*** Library of Congress. THOMAS Home. Bills, Resolutions. "Department of Peace and Nonviolence Act (Introduced in House)." http://thomas.loc.gov/cgi-bin/query/D?c110:3:./temp/~c110jcBhNs::. 5 Feb 2007.
**** Answers.com. United States Department of Defense. www.answers.com/topic/united-states-department-of-defense.

who make sacrifices for us is to be honest with them and with ourselves. The truth is that all too often we have made the decision to put them in harm's way from within the Myth. Because we are so completely unaware of alternatives to violence, I believe we give in too soon. When the Wizard tells us that he had no choice but to silence the Animals and kill Elphaba, we know there were other choices, he just couldn't conceive of them. If our government and our nation were able to live outside the Myth, would there be an end to all war? I sincerely doubt it. There will always be a point where violence becomes necessary because we will always be confronted with enemies willing and eager to use violence to destroy us.

But when we open our eyes to the futility of achieving peace through violence, we begin to seek alternative methods. Gandhi, Jesus, and Dr. Martin Luther King are among the luminaries who have lived prophetic lives to offer us an alternative path to peace. Each of these leaders insisted that violence breeds only more violence. The sad truth is that if you use violence to achieve peace, you must use more violence to maintain it. To retain his hold on power, the Wizard had to find more and more victims, silence more and more Animals and destroy any and all opposition to his "peaceful" reign. In our world, the methods of violence breed headlines like this one: "Cycle of Revenge Fuels a Pattern of Iraqi Killings."[4] The scene could be Israel/Palestine, Bosnia, the Congo or Indonesia. The century could be this one, or any other. The place or the time period doesn't matter, because the pattern is always the same. Once the violence begins, escalation is inevitable and often the side that ends the conflict is the one with the biggest weapons and the most pitiless resolve to use them. But the peace is only a temporary truce until the next faction decides it's time to use violence to make its dreams come true.

Violence changes nothing. If we can ever dare to hope for a truly peaceful world and an end to violence, we must be willing to admit that violence can never be our means for achieving such goals. M.K. Gandhi's grandson, Arun Gandhi, wrote the following passage on this subject. It was written shortly after the invasion of Iraq by coalition forces in March 2003 as a forward to a book and was posted on his website.

> For the present, there is a sense of jubilation among those who supported the war because Saddam Hussein, seen as the personification of evil, has finally been eliminated and we are told the world is now a safer place to live in. What is remarkable is the depth to which humanity allows itself to be exploited generation after generation. The one logical question that we need to ask and answer honestly is one that we keep pushing under the rug. The question is: Which of the two is a greater threat to humanity – Saddam Hussein or the culture of violence?
>
> We are told, and we accept this explanation meekly, that the Saddams and the Hitlers of the world are born evil and when they are eliminated the world becomes safer. In societies all over the world we have adopted the same system to deal with criminals. Lock them

> up or eliminate them and crime will be reduced. For generations we have been doing that but see very little impact on crime anywhere. Why is it that we blindly accept a system of dealing with conflicts that we know does not work and when it does it is just temporary? Is it because we do not want to accept the reality that true civilization of society means a radical transformation in our thinking, our behavior and our attitudes? The world successfully eliminated Hitler but was not able to eliminate the hate and prejudices that he represented. Now the world has successfully eliminated Saddam Hussein but the inhumanity that he represented will live on because we have attacked the symptom and not the malady.[5]

The malady is the belief that Good Violence exists, and eliminating this sickness will require adopting new methods of non-violence that no longer divide the world into friends and enemies, good men and evil-doers. Arun Gandhi said this about his grandfather's methods to achieve Indian independence from Great Britain:

> Gandhi never considered the British his enemies and did not allow anyone else to speak of them as enemies. He always said they are our friends and we are trying to transform their ways. This is why when India became independent India still remained on friendly terms with the British.[6]

Britain, of course, was an occupying power that had no intention of relinquishing its territory. As a colony, India was a possession, and Britain was willing to use the methods of violence to maintain its sovereignty over it. If Gandhi and his followers had considered Britain their enemy during their struggle for independence, no one would have questioned them. Instead, Gandhi chose to view Britain as a potential friend. He guided his followers to choose methods of non-violence, which always offer the possibility of transformation.

But this was a situation of unequal power – Britain controlled all the weapons and had the greater strength of armed forces. Unarmed peasants appeared to have no chance of overthrowing such a powerful nation, especially not if they chose violent means to do so. Unexpectedly, their methods of non-violence successfully toppled Britain's powerful, well-armed military forces. Their success, however, required a commitment to non-violence equivalent to the soldiers in armies of violence.

Listen to this account of a visit by Arun Gandhi to Yasser Arafat, the long-time leader of the Palestinian Liberation Army, shortly before he died. Arun pleaded with him to give up methods of violence and adopt those of non-violence as a better and more hopeful way for the Palestinians to achieve their goals of independence. The correspondent muses on the prospects:

> In fact, nonviolence is in many ways more difficult to practice than violence. Many Palestinians might die in the process, perhaps in greater numbers than they are dying now. On this point, Gandhi was clear-eyed. He and his followers were willing to die for their cause, just like the Hamas suicide bombers. Unlike the Hamas bombers, they were not willing to kill for it – under any circumstances.[7]

Those who practice non-violence are not cowards – they die in pursuit of the same stated goal as militias or terrorists do: peace and security for their people. It is not a matter of differing goals or risks, or even the number of casualties your "army" will suffer. It is a matter of methodology, and it is within these methods that the success or failure of the goal resides.

Elphaba has traveled the length of the musical to realize these truths and she has reached a decision: she no longer needs an enemy to know she is good. Fiyero's love has freed her from her need to be accepted by the Wizard, and with this freedom, her hunger for power and success within the Mythological world has melted away. As she prepares to leave Oz, she gives the Grimmerie to Glinda, hoping that she will learn how to use such knowledge for good.

Then they sing the song "For Good," which offers us a loving alternative to relationships in which everyone needs to be totally good or totally bad. Here is the entire song:

LOVE
YOUR ENEMIES

The saying attributed to Jesus, "Love your enemies and pray for those who persecute you," (Matt 5:44) has often been understood as a kind of blank check for bad guys. It seems to suggest that we reward evil-doers with our love rather than holding them accountable with our anger and the meting out of just punishments. If everyone gets love no matter how awful they are, why should anyone want to be good? Only bleeding hearts too afraid or too weak to fight would willingly stand there and be abused with a smile on their faces and love in their hearts.

Of course that (mis) understanding of the saying comes from within the Mythological world in which everyone is divided into good guys and bad guys, friends and foes. Outside the Myth, we know that our enemies are just like us, good people caught up doing bad things because of their blind adherence to the Mythological Rules. To love them means to recognize how like us they are. To love them means we will value their lives as much as we do our own. To pray for them means we hold on to the possibility of their transformation as long as we can. To live that love fully means we are willing to die for their sake, rather than to kill for our own. This saying, rather than the motto of weaklings, represents a most dangerous and risky way to live. Rather than a flowery sentiment, it is the clear-headed realism of non-violence. To live this saying requires courage, the true courage of love.

GLINDA:
I've heard it said
That people come into our lives for a reason
Bringing something we must learn
And we are led
To those who help us most to grow
If we let them
And we help them in return
Well, I don't know if I believe that's true
But I know I'm who I am today
Because I knew you

Like a comet pulled from orbit,
As it passes a sun
Like a stream that meets a boulder
Half way through the wood
Who can say if I've been changed for the better?
But, because I knew you
I have been changed for good ...

ELPHABA:
It well may be
That we will never meet again
In this lifetime
So let me say before we part
So much of me
Is made of what I learned from you
You'll be with me
Like a handprint on my heart...
And now whatever way our stories end
I know you have re-written mine
By being my friend ...
Like a ship blown from its mooring
By a wind off the sea
Like a seed dropped by a sky bird

In a distant wood
Who can say if I've been changed for the better?
But because I knew you ...

GLINDA:
Because I knew you ...

BOTH:
I have been changed for good ...

ELPHABA:
And just to clear the air
I ask forgiveness
For the things I've done you blame me for

GLINDA:
But then, I guess we know
There's blame to share

BOTH:
And none of it seems to matter anymore

GLINDA:
Like a comet pulled from orbit
As it passes a sun ...

ELPHABA:
Like a ship blown from its mooring
By a wind off the sea

GLINDA:
Like a stream that meets a boulder

ELPHABA:
Like a seed dropped by a bird

GLINDA:
Halfway through the wood

ELPHABA:
In the wood

BOTH:
Who can say if I've been changed for the better?
I do believe I have been changed for the better

GLINDA:
And because I knew you ...

ELPHABA:
Because I knew you ...

BOTH:
Because I knew you
I have been changed for good.

Glinda and Elphaba's friendship becomes full and complete at the moment when they accept each other's differences. Glinda will never have Elphaba's powers, skill to interpret the Grimmerie, or Fiyero's love, but none of that matters anymore. Elphaba will never have Glinda's charm, or the political or leadership skills she possesses, but what difference does that make now? Each has been open and vulnerable to the other and as a result, forever changed by the friendship, "like a handprint on my heart."

Now that's a new way to live. Why be "good" when you can be loving? Glinda and Elphaba have shattered the Myth told about good and evil by redefining the terms. Good is not being perfect or popular. It is being honest about your failings and open to the influence of others. It is accepting limits on your behavior and repenting your mistakes. And evil is not who or what someone else says it is, but a failure to love.

The cyclone that L. Frank Baum gave us is a wonderful metaphor for what happens to life when we devote ourselves to being good on the Myth's terms. We end up eternally seeking enemies to defeat, while accepting no limits on our behavior. Life becomes an endless cycle of accusation leading to accusation, our vision blinded so that we cannot see the damage we leave in our wake. Choosing instead to love, forgive and repent deserves a different metaphor than the destructive cyclone of the Myth. Life lived within the limits of Unconditional Love is better represented by a tiny, ever-widening circle, like the ripple made by a pebble in a pond. At first small and narrow, our capacity to love seems unimportant, barely able to make an impact on the waters. But with each loving act we take, with each courageous move toward repentance, the circle grows wider and wider, eventually reaching the very banks of the pond. Love works to expand its boundaries, to include more and more people within its embrace, even the wicked, even our enemies, even ourselves.

Sadly for Elphaba and Fiyero, their knowledge of the Myth comes from the position of victim. They are Oz's scapegoats, and when faced with the threat of lynching at the hands of an angry mob, discretion is indeed the better part of valor. The only safe place for victims is in another country altogether. To ensure their safety, they cannot tell anyone where they are going, not even Glinda. In fact, it's probably better for Glinda that she does not possess such knowledge – it would compromise her too much. Glinda watches as the mob appears to corner Elphaba and destroy her, but Glinda does not see what the audience sees – that both Elphaba and Fiyero have survived the assault. We are happy for them, but our happiness is tainted by the knowledge that the friends may never see each other again and that Glinda will not have even the hope of a reunion that Elphaba can cling to.

With the Grimmerie in hand and her heart heavy with grief, Glinda confronts both Morrible and the Wizard. She doesn't demonize them or celebrate their downfall, but she demands that they abdicate their positions of power and accept the consequences of their misdeeds. Morrible is sent to prison and Glinda does seem to enjoy wielding the power in their relationship for a change. But it is hopeful that Glinda does not let herself become consumed by anger or revenge. Holding the two of them accountable is revenge enough.

We also discover, along with Glinda, that Elphaba's father was not Frex, but the Wizard himself. When he learns that he has brought about the demise of his own child, the Wizard collapses in grief. Rather than reap a harvest of goodness, the methods promoted by the Myth inevitably lead to the destruction of the relationships we hold most dear. This secret holds the key to one more discovery about who Elphaba is – daughter to a master of deceit, the emperor of a kingdom built on lies, the founder of a peace bought at the expense of innocent victims.

Elphaba's struggle to free herself from the influence of such a father is a metaphor for the journey away from Mythological thinking. Although she was not aware of her true paternity, Elphaba shared many characteristics with the Wizard. Like the Wizard, she believed in the Mythological Rules and did her best to be good within the Sacrificial System. We also have such a secret parent, like Elphaba. We, too, are ignorant of our "paternity," of our origins and upbringing within a culture built on lies. And like Elphaba, our initial steps out of that culture involve trying to be good on the Myth's terms.

The path to true goodness will lead us away from such a father. It will take courage and cause us much suffering, but it will bring us to a new place where true happiness and peace are possible. Morrible makes an insightful comment when Elphaba's relationship to the Wizard is revealed. She says, "That's it! That's why she had such power! She was a child of both worlds!" We, too, can be children of both worlds – we can become fully aware of how the Myth works and expertly equipped to navigate its threats. As we reject the ways of mythological culture, we will be able to see innocence in our victims and examine our own needs and fears. Our need to be good will be overpowered by our need to do good, and our fears will be transformed into hope and peace.

But there is still work to do before the curtain falls. Glinda has the mob to deal with. She faces the crowd caught up in the thrall of the Myth, still celebrating the death of the Wicked Witch. Glinda addresses them:

GLINDA:
Fellow Ozians, friends, we have been through a frightening time. And there will be other times and other things that frighten us. But if you let me, I'd like to try to help. I'd like to try to be ... Glinda the Good.

OZIANS:
Good News!!

Glinda's desire to be truly good gives us hope. The Ozians have a new leader now, someone who is completely free of the Myth told of good and evil. For the first time, we are hopeful that they may one day sing with new understanding and will become capable of living and proclaiming truly good news for every citizen of Oz.

14

The Murky Grey Road

I object to violence because when it appears to do good, the good is only temporary; the evil it does is permanent.

MAHATMA GANDHI (1869 – 1948)

The important thing was to love rather than to be loved.

W. SOMERSET MAUGHAM, *Of Human Bondage*

Now that we have heard the story of the Wicked Witch of the West, our response to her death is forever changed. From now on, when we reach the end of the 1939 movie, rather than celebrate with Dorothy and her friends, we may shed a tear for the sad fate that befell the lonely, green Elphaba. Her story has opened our eyes to the ways in which we used her for our own ends. We may feel ashamed that we identified with Dorothy and her friends, that we favorably compared our goodness to the Witch's wickedness, or that we took comfort in knowing all of Oz was safe from evil upon her destruction.

The discomfort we feel now when we hear a story of good conquering evil is a sign that we are on the path toward a new way of life. Our new worldview is so utterly different from the old, that I'm tempted to use the phrase "born again" to describe it. We find that what once gave meaning to our lives has been revealed as nothing more than shadowy lies, dependent on the oppression of others. Thanks to Glinda's courageous tale of Elphaba's background, we have been given a glimpse of a world anchored in compassion over abuse, in joy over suffering and in peace over violence.

We know that good people do bad things, and that one bad act does not rule out all goodness. But the Myth polarizes all individuals with absolute certainty: good and bad cannot coexist in the same person. In the Myth, a good person is like a glass of water and a bad deed like red food coloring – one drop and the entire glass of water is contaminated, forever altered. *Wicked* has revealed the truth that a bad deed is more like a red marble dropped into that glass – it disturbs the water but does not alter the nature of the water forever. The marble can be removed and the water restored to its original state. This is one way to begin to see the good and bad in everyone. Where there is room for change, we can face the unintentional harm our attempts to be good may be causing others. This view forces us to see that all of us have a marble or two in our glass.

We know that the tendency for good people to accumulate a few marbles – and steadfastly deny it – is not confined to fairy tale landscapes. The particular kind of marbles we are concerned with here, of course, represent false accusations of wickedness and the accompanying blindness to the suffering it causes. In our own world we have always needed Wicked Witches, people who could bear the burden of evil so we could feel good. The true path to goodness will lead us outside of the Myth to an entirely new world, where goodness is defined by our willingness to admit that good people sometimes make bad decisions. In this world, good people see evil in themselves, goodness in their enemies and mourn the death of witches.

The path that leads beyond the Myth is not made of yellow brick. As you begin to journey down it, you will long for the shining clarity you used to have about good and evil. Unlike the road that led to the Emerald City, this road is murky grey, and has many forks and dead ends. On this road, nothing is certain, and you must be able to balance the strength of your convictions with a healthy respect for the convictions of others. On this road you have to be willing to test your beliefs, ask for directions, retrace your steps, and make wrong turns. But those individuals brave enough to take the journey will find they are on the road to a remarkable possibility. They will discover that they are laying the foundation not for a city of illusions, but a city of truth, whose peace is authentic, inclusive and lasting.

The path out of the Myth is not completely devoid of landmarks. In fact, it is filled with them: They are the Wicked Witches of our world, the ones that each of us harbors in our hearts as enemy, evil, or "other." Is your Wicked Witch someone whom you cannot respond to except in hate and anger – an absent father, an abusive mother, a disloyal friend, an ex-spouse, a disappointing child, a manipulative co-worker, a failed idol? Is there an entire group of people that inspires you to fear or rage? Perhaps it's Mexican immigrants, African-Americans, welfare recipients or the homeless, the mentally ill or physically handicapped, criminals or terrorists, Republicans or Democrats, lawyers or politicians, environmentalists or Creationists, faiths outside of yours – Islam, Judaism, liberal Christianity, conservative Christianity, Hinduism, Buddhism, atheism, agnosticism, secular humanism?

Who is it that you demonize? Whose story do you refuse to hear? The list of potential scapegoats is endless, of course, because it includes anyone who is different than we are, or anyone whom we cannot find it in our hearts to forgive. What we do when we encounter these landmarks, these "witches," tells us which road we are on – the Myth's road of yellow brick, or the pothole-riddled road to peace. Do you stop and listen to the story of your enemy, taking the risk that such a pause entails? *Wicked* has made clear that the response of peace requires the courage to listen to the story of your wicked witch.

Unfortunately, the courage to listen to our scapegoats is incredibly difficult to muster. Which is why I am forever grateful to the writers and producers of *Wicked* for offering us such an entertaining invitation into the hidden world of the victims of Mythological thinking. The delightful experience of the musical opens our hearts so that we are able to deal with the questions that we would rather avoid asking about our enemies:

JUDGE NOT

In the Christian scriptures, Jesus is quoted as saying not to judge or you will also be judged. What did he mean by that? Here is the exact quote:

> Do not judge, and you will not be judged; do not condemn, and you will not be condemned. Forgive, and you will be forgiven; give and it will be given to you. (Luke 6:37-38)

I've always had a hard time with this concept, because it didn't make sense to me. How can God who is supposed to represent goodness ask me not to judge the difference between good and evil actions, friendships and activities? After all, isn't life all about judging, making choices and decisions? How exactly am I supposed to be good if I judge not?

All those questions originate within the Myth, but Jesus was speaking from outside of the Myth. He was counseling against judgments of the Mythological kind which say "I'll love you, if ..." and always include a threat of condemnation. They are the calculating kind of judgments made by Galinda when she decides whom she will love based on what they can do for her. They are the judgments of the Wizard as he decides who will be in his government based on what he can gain from them politically, rather than the good they can do the nation. And they are the judgments we make with absolute certainty when we locate and condemn our scapegoats.

Outside the Myth, this sort of judging – a better word might be calculating – has no place. Rather than judging and condemning, Jesus advocates forgiveness and generosity. Judging and condemning are the tools of scapegoating. Forgiveness and generosity are the tools of lasting peace. This saying cautions us that if we judge and condemn we will build communities in which we will be at risk of being a scapegoat. Forgive and give freely, and we will build communities in which scapegoats are not needed and we are loved for who we are, not for what someone can gain from us.

Do we derive our sense of goodness by accusing someone else of being evil?

Do we turn a blind eye to the suffering we cause others?

Are our enemies no more evil than we are?

Recently I saw this headline in The Wall Street Journal: "A Few Centuries Late, Convicted Witches Gain New Defenders." The story was about the descendant of a convicted witch who was executed in 1647 with about a dozen others in Connecticut. The descendant of the executed woman is working to get legislation passed and signed by the Governor that would exonerate her ancestor. She has reason to be hopeful. Already the governors of Virginia and Massachusetts have done as much for citizens of their states. And in 2004, 81 people (along with their cats!) were pardoned for witchcraft in the small town of Prestonpans, Scotland.[1]

Why is it that 400 years ago, so many moral people, acting in the name of goodness, could be so blind? Even today, people completely trapped inside the Myth have no trouble seeing that the accused witches were functioning as scapegoats, allowing the community to believe that they were good people while bringing them a sense of unity and peace at the expense of the "witches." The understanding of what a scapegoat is and how it functions is working its way into our popular culture. Even though the prevailing Myth is still one of Good and Bad Violence, we can now catch glimpses of the truth that the Myth is concealing. We can see, sometimes more clearly than at other times, when a person or group is being scapegoated.

Historical examples like the one involving the witches are easy for us. We can easily see innocent people behind the accusations and occasionally we can even see innocence in contemporary situations. I believe progress has been made, but there is obviously more work yet to be accomplished. The truth is, we are getting better and better at seeing scapegoating *when someone else is doing it*. The danger with historical examples is that we believe that we are somehow different than our ancestors, that we would never make the same mistakes. But the next ethical advance that awaits humanity, I believe, is to admit our similarities with the witch hunters of the 1600's and those in the musical. The one group of people in the musical with whom no one identifies is the Ozian mob. The question that challenges both the inhabitants of Oz and the readers of this book is the same, and is the only way to escape the Myth: How do we identify our own scapegoats?

When we take action against an identified evil, we believe in ourselves as defenders of the public good, champions of justice, liberty and truth. Our sense of ourselves as good people is so married to finding evil with absolute certainty that if someone suggests that we may be mistaken in our accusations, they risk becoming the targets of our wrath. It is the risk that Glinda takes by telling Elphaba's story to the Ozian mob. From within our world, I'd like to offer the example of two men who dared to take similar risks.

The first is the pastor of an evangelical megachurch, Rev. Gregory A. Boyd. His church is in suburban St. Paul, Minnesota, where he often receives requests to endorse conservative political candidates and their causes from the pulpit. He refuses every time. Finally, fed up with the number of requests he was fielding, he preached a series of six sermons on the risks of the church becoming politicized, or morally triumphant, or consumed by patriotic fervor. Mr. Boyd insists that he is not a liberal, though he preached that, "When the church wins the culture wars, it inevitably loses. When it conquers the world it becomes the world. When you put your trust in the sword, you lose the cross." Bravely, he continued, "I am sorry to tell you that America is not the light of the world and the hope of the world. The light of the world and the hope of the world is Jesus Christ."[2]

Now, whether you are theologically liberal, conservative, or entirely secular, step back from those identities for just a moment and imagine how it feels to be told that the good things you think you are doing – voting for the best candidate, defending the weak or powerless, standing up for ethical and moral standards and doing God's work – are actually bad things. And someone who epitomizes morality and service to others is telling you these things. You can imagine the reaction he received. Here is how it was reported in the newspaper:

> The response from his congregation ... was passionate. Some members walked out of a sermon and never returned. By the time the dust had settled, Woodland Hills, which Mr. Boyd founded in 1992, had lost about 1,000 of its 5,000 members ... Some pastors in his denomination, the Baptist General conference, mounted an effort to evict Mr. Boyd from the denomination and his teaching post, but he won the battle.[3]

Unless you think this is a problem only conservative churches face, listen to the story of what happened in my small, liberal congregation a few years ago. We had a long history of political activism as a congregation. Members marched in civil rights protests, in the 1980's we became a Sanctuary Church offering safe haven to political refugees from Latin America in defiance of the U.S. government's policy, and we became an open and affirming church, actively welcoming gay and lesbian congregants. Of course, each time we voted to take such a position, we lost a large percentage of the congregation because members would walk out rather than stay and participate in a cause they felt uncomfortable supporting.

Then we called a new pastor, Rev. C. David Owens, who refused to preach or endorse any political issues from the pulpit. Members requested repeatedly over the years that he direct the congregation to take stands on issues from the environment to economic policy to the Gulf War. His answer was always the same: We are not taking up and down votes on politically charged issues anymore. Who was he to tell people how to respond to God's call? He felt his job was to preach and teach the truths found in scripture. It was the job of the parishioners to discern how that truth would be translated into their lives. Needless to say, many members were disappointed yet again.

Rev. Owens lasted for a few years before his personal life became a disappointment to them as well. Some of the politically active members accused him of being unfit for the ministry and one group made an effort to have him stripped of his credentials by our denomination, the United Church of Christ. People who worshipped together each Sunday and had been friends for years were forced to take sides. Hearts were broken, trusts betrayed and friendships shattered beyond repair. Rev. Owens won the battle, but we lost many members. Our congregation is just now beginning to recover from the deep wounds of broken friendships.

What happened in these two congregations, so different politically, yet identical in their patterns of internal conflict? Both congregations had taken their sense of identity from their moral stances and political positions. In so doing, they had become dependent on their enemies to define themselves. Whether you are for a particular war or against it, pro-life or pro-choice, approving of homosexuality or disapproving, you have set up an opposition between yourself and some "other" who is, by virtue of their opposite position, your enemy. When someone tries to deprive you of that enemy, your entire sense of being is threatened. The need for the enemy is so strong, that the one who is calling your attention to that need must be eliminated. By daring to call their congregations on their scapegoating behavior, both pastors became scapegoats themselves.

When an individual or group becomes your enemy, you have permission to refuse to listen to them. Liberals and conservatives each have their own news outlets on television, radio and in print, and rarely do they tune in to the other's conversation. What's interesting about the two congregations is that, though they are geographically miles apart and personally unfamiliar to each other, ideologically they represent the "enemy" to the other. Each congregation had become insular and disdainful of the political stance represented by its opposition. It would be hard to imagine these congregations saying anything nice about the other, as they each claim to occupy the moral, Christian high ground. Yet they behaved identically – with anger and aggression – when confronted by their pastors.

Lest my secular readers become too self-satisfied with their decision to avoid religious communities, there are many examples from the secular world in which the majority reacted with anger when forced to listen to the voices of their victims. The most famous in our time is Dr. Martin Luther King, who was jailed, investigated, and threatened by our government, and finally killed for confronting this nation's attitude toward its racial minorities. Two other well-known examples are Aung San Suu Kyi and Nelson Mandela, also Nobel Peace Prize laureates.

Aung San Suu Kyi is an oppositional leader and human rights advocate who uses non-violent methods to fight for democratic change against the totalitarian and repressive regime in her country, Burma. She was under house arrest at the time she received her Nobel Prize. Here is what the presenter of the prize, Francis Sejersted, Chairman of the Norwegian Nobel Committee, said about her at the ceremony she could not attend:

> In the good fight for peace and reconciliation, we are dependent on persons who set examples, persons who can symbolise what we are seeking and mobilise the best in us. Aung San Suu Kyi is just such a person. She unites deep commitment and tenacity with a vision in which the end and the means form a single unit. Its most important elements are: democracy, respect for human rights, reconciliation between groups, non-violence, and personal and collective discipline.[4]

She was released in 1995 after six years but continues to be under constant government surveillance.

Nelson Mandela, the 1993 Nobel Peace Prize winner from South Africa, was jailed from 1962 till his release in 1990. At the time of his conviction Mandela said:

> I have fought against white domination, and I have fought against black domination. I have cherished the ideal of a democratic and free society in which all persons live together in harmony and with equal opportunities. It is an ideal which I hope to live for and to achieve. But if needs be, it is an ideal for which I am prepared to die.[5]

Both of these leaders have dared to confront governments that willingly sacrifice the few for the many in order to maintain control of their power. Of course, these are but a small sampling of heroic people who have dared to speak out, but both demonstrate that the issues are widespread. The impulse to scapegoat is not a religious-versus-secular issue, a conservative-versus-liberal issue, or U.S.-versus-other nations issue. It's not even a good-versus-evil issue. It is a "versus" issue. It's about how we define our goodness and the evil of our enemies. Pitting ourselves as opposite some starkly different "other" allows us to sanctify our own violence and hatred while demonizing that of our opponents. We become so convinced that there is Good Violence and Bad Violence, that we cannot see how the use of violence erases the differences we so desperately wish to assert between ourselves and our perceived enemies.

There is even some speculation today on the part of researchers that our brains may be hardwired in a way that allows us to think the best of our own actions and the worst of others. A recent study from the University of Texas[6] indicates that we view our own violent behavior as a response to provocation, but that we view the violent behavior of others as unprovoked. This exists across cultures, for all societies seem to prohibit violent behavior except when it is a response to someone else's violence against them. The second punch is always viewed as morally superior to the first one. Another study conducted at the University College London illustrates this quite well. Here's how it was described:

> The researcher began the game by exerting a fixed amount of pressure on the first volunteer's finger. The first volunteer was then asked to exert precisely the same amount of pressure on the second volunteer's finger. The second volunteer was then asked to exert the same amount of pressure on the first volunteer's finger. And so on. The two volunteers took turns applying equal amounts of pressure to each other's fingers while the researchers measured the actual amount of pressure they applied.
>
> The results were striking. Although volunteers tried to respond to each other's touches with equal force, they typically responded with about 40 percent more force than they had just experienced. Each time a volunteer was touched, he touched back harder, which led the other volunteer to touch back even harder. What began as a game of soft touches quickly became a game of moderate pokes and then hard prods, even though both volunteers were doing their level best to respond in kind.
>
> Each volunteer was convinced that he was responding with equal force and that for some reason the other volunteer was

THERE ARE NONE SO BLIND AS THOSE WHO WILL NOT SEE

In America, we are currently experiencing what if feels like to be the victims of destructive evil. The forces of the extreme fundamentalist* group Al Queda claim that we are evil, and so they feel free to kill us without any moral misgivings. Al Queda refuses to listen to us no matter how we try to explain that we harbor no evil intentions against them or their people, we simply want to live in peace. Yet, when Al Queda kills Americans it is a cause for celebration as if we are less than human, more like fairy tale witches to be gleefully incinerated than real people whose death would be considered a tragedy. Here is a posting from an extremist website that often posts Al Queda material. It was published on the fifth anniversary of the September 11 attacks.

> Before my eyes is a veil that does not permit me to see those killed in the twin towers, nor to remember them on this day. Indeed, I don't see those killed in the twin towers ... Do you know why?
>
> Because their fallen are not purer or better than our fallen. And because the blood of my Muslim brothers and that of my family in Palestine ... and in Iraq and in Afghanistan and in every location in which Muslim blood is shed has blocked my vision ... filled my retinas with black lines so that I can see only our martyrs and injured being slain by America's weapons ...

While we might recoil at this callousness, we can also learn from its revealing imagery. The writer says that his rage over the suffering of his people has literally blinded him. Not only does he choose not to see our suffering, his retinas are so affected that he cannot see it despite his gaze being turned in our direction. This blindness is a hallmark of those caught up in the Myth. It is what allows this man to value some lives more highly than others, giving justification to the indiscriminate killing of Americans at the same time that he grieves the deaths of Muslims.

...continued on next page

...continued from previous page

While our first concern as Americans is to protect ourselves and our nation against such heartless violence, we would do well to also protect ourselves against becoming similarly afflicted with blindness. If we do not guard against it, we will lose our ability, as this man has done, to tell the difference between the truly evil and the falsely accused. My grandfather would often quote an old English proverb when I stubbornly refused to admit that I had done something wrong. He would say, "Suzanne, there are none so blind as those who will not see." Deliberate blindness, like a disease, afflicts the good and the bad alike. Its most dangerous symptom is the inability to see the immorality of your own violence.

* The term "fundamentalist" refers to a movement or strain of faith that exists across religions. According to Karen Armstrong, "Fundamentalism is a global fact and has surfaced in every major faith in response to the problems of our modernity." Armstrong explains that there is fundamentalism in Judaism, Christianity, Islam, Hinduism, Buddhism, Sikhism and Confucianism. All fundamentalist movements share "a deep disappointment and disenchantment with the modern experiment... [and] express real fear... that the secular establishment is determined to wipe them out." Armstrong comments that, "This is not always a paranoid reaction." Karen Armstrong (2000) *Islam, A Short History*. (New York, NY: Random House) 164-165.

** Bernard Haykel and Saud al-Sarhan, "The Apocalypse Will Be Blogged," New York Times. 12 Sept. 2006: A25.

escalating. Neither realized that the escalation was the natural byproduct of a neurological quirk that causes the pain we receive to seem more painful than the pain we produce, so we usually give more pain than we have received.[7]

Could it be that there is a biological predisposition to being blind to the pain we cause others? Is it harder to understand someone else's suffering than it is to blame them for causing ours? If that is true, then the task of learning to identify our own scapegoats is a difficult one indeed. Though not impossible.

Psychologists have done studies that appear to prove the existence of empathy in rhesus monkeys. In one such study, the monkeys were trained to pull chains to receive different amounts of food, one yielding half as much as the other. The researchers then changed the result for pulling the chain with more food – now each time they pulled the chain another monkey in their sight received a shock. After witnessing the distress of another monkey, two-thirds of the experimental subjects pulled the non-shock chain even though it resulted in half as much food. A summary of the experiment reported that, "Of the remaining third, one stopped pulling the chains altogether for 5 days and another for 12 days after witnessing the shock of the object. These monkeys were literally starving themselves to prevent the shock" to the other monkey. Two factors appeared to increase the probability that a monkey would rather starve himself than risk harming another – actually seeing the result of the shock and familiarity with the sufferer.[8]

How interesting and similar to what happened to Glinda in the musical. The more Glinda got to know Elphaba and witnessed her suffering, the more she was able to act out of concern for her rather than out of self-interest. It is this possibility for empathy that the Myth is desperate to circumvent. By keeping us blind to our victim's suffering, it ensures that we will keep pulling on the chain of self-interest rather than choose self-sacrifice and leave behind the ways of the Sacrificial System. I do believe that human beings share a great capacity to perceive the emotional and physical suffering of others, however, the Myth blinds us to the suffering of our victims, and our empathy is suppressed in favor of our tendency to retaliate and escalate.

The movie, *A History of Violence*, is an attempt to call our attention to our culture's dependency on violence to achieve the peace it enjoys. I am relying on an interpretation of the film offered by James K.A. Smith, Associate Professor of Philosophy at Calvin College in Grand Rapids, Michigan[9]. The action takes place within a loving, peaceful family that begins to realize that their father is a former hit man and killer. The gruesome action of the movie follows the father's attempts to resist the call to return to his former life, all the while committing acts of violence as his method of resistance. In the end, after committing multiple murders, he returns to his family who silently welcomes him to the dinner table as if they never learned of his capacity to kill. This is how Prof. Smith analyzes the final scene:

> ...his silent welcome to the table at home is not a matter of eucharistic hospitality and forgiveness, but rather the silent complacency that wants to act *as if* we weren't implicated, *as if* we can just get on with our lives and not talk about it. At the heart of this reading is a heightened sense of the banality of violence – that the pristine peace of every Mayberry is built upon a history of violence.[10]

The musical *Wicked* and our own sense of compassion are summoning us to an awareness of our complicity in violence. Can we learn to live without scapegoats? Can we find another way to achieve happiness and peace that does not willingly and blithely sacrifice the happiness and peace of others? I believe we can if we are willing to talk about it. If we are willing to give up living *as if* nothing is happening beneath the surface and behind the scenes, I believe we can begin to travel the murky grey road in search of the true city of peace.

Undertaking such a journey will demand that we live according to a new creed, The Creed of Compassion. The Creed of Self-Worship permits and condones the use of scapegoats. This new creed offers us a new way of conceiving of our desires and ourselves:

CREED OF COMPASSION

- I am limited.
- True peace is universal peace.
- Violence or the abuse of another human being can never be justified.

By accepting limits to our behavior (no scapegoating allowed), we refuse to use and abuse others for any purpose, even the fulfillment of our own desires. When we refuse to accept peace for ourselves unless it is for everyone (even scapegoats), it is then that we become fulfilled and find our happy ending.

This Creed places limits on the fulfillment of our desires and by so doing actually redefines personal desire. How? Interestingly, both Creeds offer the same reward for following them – happiness. The Creed of Self-Worship says that your own happiness can be bought at the expense of someone else's. There are no limits on what you may desire or on the methods you can employ. The Creed of Compassion says that personal happiness is only realized when others are happy, too. Interesting, isn't it? This Creed actually limits our desires by redefining them in terms of the happiness of others. If others are happy, it says, then we will be happy, too. Truly happy.

Is it possible to follow such a Creed? The musical offers six ways to live outside the Myth, and for each we will examine both the benefits and the costs. Be aware that we ourselves will pay all the costs – this new Creed will not tolerate someone else paying the price for our peace and happiness.

LIVING THE WICKED TRUTH

1. LEARN TO LOVE GREY

The new Creed asks that we let go of hard and fast categories of good and evil in favor of the common bond of our humanity. It insists that we recognize the similarities we share with one another, as well as our enemies. To do so, we will need to be honest with ourselves about our own failings (that's a cost of the Creed), yet still find a way to love and accept ourselves – imperfections and all. As we rooted for Elphaba to love her green skin, so must we cheer ourselves on in those dark moments when we despair of our own worthiness. If we can love ourselves in spite of our faults, we may not need to turn others into hateful witches. This is what makes the road to peace so murky – rather than affixing people into black and white categories of good and evil, we recognize that we exist within shades of grey. Scapegoating is much more difficult when we recognize the capacity we all share for good and evil.

2. LEARN TO TELL THE TRUTH FROM THE LIE

There are interconnected lies that the Myth wants us to believe: (1) There is Good Violence, and (2) the end justifies the means. When we understand that all violence is bad and that the means become the end, we will recognize all types of lies throughout contemporary society. We see the lie in the culture of consumerism with its slick advertisements proclaiming that our happiness depends on accumulating objects, buying into the latest fad. We see the lie in reality television, which celebrates passing judgment on others and voting them out of your community as a form of entertainment. And everywhere we turn we see violence portrayed as a harmless or legitimate weapon in the arsenal for good. The lie lives in the politics of negation and hate, violent movies and video games, weapons called "peacemakers" and leaders who glorify violence over peace talks. When we encounter anyone, whether they are a dear friend or an elected official, who insists that one person or group of people is the cause of all our problems, and our only choice is to eliminate them, we are being told a lie.

The cost is that before we can change we must accept our own participation in this system that has promoted and encouraged suffering. This is very painful and many would rather renew their support for the ways of the Myth than admit that they have been wrong. Admitting to our own mistakes is perhaps the most difficult truth to tell.

3. PRACTICE SELF-GIVING LOVE

Even pretend acts of love can transform destructive relationships into friendships. Rather than return hate for hate, the Creed of Compassion asks us to try returning love even in the most hateful situations. There may not be an immediate change, but our hearts and spirit will be transformed in the effort, and that may be enough.

The cost of such a vulnerable practice is that you may get hurt. Others may climb ahead of you on the corporate ladder or take advantage of you in relationships. But the Creed asks that we make this choice with our eyes and hearts wide open, rather than ask others to pay the price for us.

4. FORGIVE

The only way that it is possible to return love for hate is if we can find it in our hearts not to hold grudges. If we can remember that we are as much in need of forgiveness as those whom we call our enemies, we can gain the compassion necessary to see things from another perspective. Many people will argue that the cost of this practice will be bad deeds gone unpunished. But that is not what forgiveness is. Forgiveness always holds people accountable for their deeds – the very act of saying "I forgive" is an acknowledgement that someone has done something wrong.

Forgiveness is not about giving someone a free pass. People must be held accountable for their bad deeds, but the only way to free yourself from the cycle of hatred is to practice forgiveness. Otherwise, you risk believing that the violence perpetrated against you was bad while the violence you allow is good. You will be caught up in a cycle of revenge, rather than in the search for transformation. When you are consumed with the desire to punish, be on your guard – for that may well be a sign that you are about to exercise violence in the belief that it is good. Punishing a perpetrator may make us feel good about ourselves, but it does little to end the threat of evil.

In fact, punishment more often entrenches the evil than alleviates it. It fuels fury rather than sows community. Only by grounding our response in love, can we conquer hate. Forgiveness also frees you from dependence on your abuser for healing. It frees you from a victim identity. There is a story in the gospel of Matthew about a time when Jesus was teaching about forgiveness and the disciples were wondering if there were limits on it. They wanted to know how many times they had to forgive someone who hurt them and offered seven as a good number. By then, the offender must surely have responded to the forgiveness with repentance and a change of heart. If not, they were no longer worthy of forgiveness. But Jesus answered, "Not seven times, but, I tell you, seven times seventy." (Matt 18:22) In other words, there is no limit on forgiveness. It is not something you can do IF or IN ORDER TO get a result in return, like repentance or an apology. You forgive because forgiveness is not about the perpetrator, but about the one who has been wounded. When you continue to hold a grudge, you are caught up in a victim identity – you know who you are because you are not that hateful person who hurt you and yet you need that person's love and approval even though you can never get it. Forgiveness allows you to move away from a victim identity into a place where you are healed of the harm done to you and free to move forward into a new, positive sense of self. This is an altogether new way of releasing anger and aggression – rather than seeking a scapegoat, the Creed of Compassions asks that we seek a change of heart.

5. REALIZE THAT YOU HAVE SCAPEGOATS

This may be the most difficult of all. As we have discussed, it is very hard to see your own scapegoats and very easy to see someone else's. In fact, the moment you recognize that you have a scapegoat, you cease to have one. Rather than wicked people, they become victims of persecution – yours. To live within the new Creed, we must live within a community we can trust to help identify our scapegoats for us and then be open to hearing their insights.

The cost is that we will have to find a new way to deal with our anger and resentments. We will also have to find a community that supports our new vision, that understands our stance against violence and scapegoating, and who can share an honest perspective on our actions. This may necessitate letting go of toxic relationships, bitter friendships and associations that fuel our former self. Adopting a community committed to love and a practice of forgiveness will lead to a reduction in hatred, anger, and the need for scapegoats.

6. MOURN THE WICKED

If we have exhausted all options, and must resort to the use of violence, it can never be a cause of celebration. The use of violence means that we have failed to transform the situation through love and compassion. Even those who behave wickedly are human and their deaths can never be celebrated, for we must acknowledge that we have killed a person, not a monster or a witch. We must mourn the times when we resort to violence to defeat evil to protect others or ourselves.

The cost? We will have given up our easy solution to the problem of evil and will have to find another way besides scapegoating and violence to bring peace. It is a difficult occupation, but it is worthy of a lifetime's commitment.

Theologian James Alison talks about what it means to be a Christian this way: "The Christianity lies not in the being right or being wrong, but in the helping each other out of the hole."[11] We can rephrase Alison by saying, "*Being good* lies not in the being right or being wrong, but in the helping each other out of the hole." What is that hole? Belief in the Myth, belief that the end justifies the means, belief in sacrificing the one for the many, belief in the concept of Good Violence. When do good people do bad things? When they get trapped inside the Myth and can't find a way out. Then they can commit all manner of hurtful acts without ever feeling guilty, because the hurt is hidden, the victim silenced. Helping each other out of the hole is the way of true goodness.

The musical opened with the refrain, "No one mourns the Wicked." We can amend that now. The truth is that no one who believes in the Myth mourns the wicked. Once you have stepped outside of the Myth and are no longer blinded by the smokescreen of lies, it becomes very difficult to join the celebration of someone's death, no matter how wicked the world believed her to be. Once you see what the Myth wants to hide, every celebration of every death has a cautionary note for you, for behind every accusation of wickedness you have to wonder, is there a powerless little man hoping to be a wonderful wizard or an angry and resentful community looking for a scapegoat? And might the wickedest witch of all be a lonely green girl who only wants to be loved?

Living by the Creed of Compassion will not be easy. It requires that we give up our need for certainty, for knowing absolutely, without a doubt who is good and who is evil. The irony is, of course, that once we let go of our need to be good, we will be better than we have ever been. Once we let go of needing someone else to be evil, we will be astounded at the discoveries we make about the true nature and location of evil. Once we let the story of Glinda and Elphaba transform us like "a handprint on [our] heart," we will be able to sing with them, "I have been changed for good."

ENDNOTES

CHAPTER 1

1. *Wicked*. Prod. Marc Platt. Musical. Universal Pictures, the Araca Group, Jon B. Platt, and David Stone, 2003.
2. Music and lyrics by Stephen Schwartz, book by Winnie Holzman. All material used by permission of the authors.
3. *The Wizard of Oz.* Dir. Victor Fleming. Perf. Judy Garland. Film. MGM Studios, 1939.
4. *Ibid.*
5. Gregory Maguire, *Wicked: The Life and Times of the Wicked Witch of the West* (New York: Regan Books/Harper Collins, 1995).
6. L. Frank Baum, *The Wonderful Wizard of Oz* (New York: Sterling Publishing Co., Inc., 2005).
7. Baum, 156.
8. Baum, 22.
9. Baum, 83.
10. Baum, 74.
11. Baum, 90.
12. Baum, 100.

CHAPTER 2

1. James Bond, Terminator, Die Hard and Mission: Impossible: Release dates, production companies and additional information is available at www.imdb.com.
2. This understanding of myth was popularized by the writer and lecturer, Joseph Campbell. He published a series of books on the subject and was featured on the series, *Moyers: Joseph Campbell and the Power of Myth.* PBS,1988. He was Professor Emeritus at Sarah Lawrence College until his death in 1987.
3. David Cote, *Wicked: The Grimmerie* (Melcher Media, New York: Hyperion, 2005) 19-20.
4. *Ibid.*
5. *Ibid.*
6. René Girard, *Job: The Victim of His People*, trans. Yvonne Freccero (Stanford, CA: Stanford University Press, 1987) 34.
7. Wickipedia, The Free Encyclopedia. "Lynching in the United States." http://en.wikipedia.org/wiki/Lynching_in_the_United_States.

CHAPTER 3

1. Cote, 76.
2. Girard, *Job* 123.

CHAPTER 4

1. George Donelson Moss, *America in the Twentieth Century* (Upper Saddle River, New Jersey: Prentice Hall, 2000) 112.
2. Hitler, Adolf. Mein Kampf (Boston: Houghton Mifflin, 1939) 920.

CHAPTER 5

1. René Girard, *Violence and Sacred*, trans. Patrick Gregory (Baltimore, MD: Johns Hopkins University Press, 1977) 92. Italics are Girard's. Original publication: *La Violence et le Sacré,* (Paris, France: Editions Bernard Grasset, 1972).
2. *Ibid*, 94.
3. *True Lies.* Dir. James Cameron. Film. Perfs. Arnold Schwarzenneger, Jamie Lee Curtis. Boss Film Studios, 1994.
4. Panel discussion, "Mimesis Creativity and Reconciliation," *Colloquium on Violence & Religion Conference*. Ottawa, Canada. 31 May – 4 Jun. 2006.
5. James G. Williams, ed. *The Girard Reader* (New York, NY: A Crossroad Herder Book, Crossroad Publishing Company, 1996) 15.

CHAPTER 7

1. Girard, *Job* 13.

CHAPTER 8

1. James Alison, *The Joy of Being Wrong: Original Sin Through Easter Eyes* (New York, NY: A Herder & Herder Book, Crossroad Publishing Company) 1998.
2. Alison, 80.

CHAPTER 9

1. Marlise Simons, "Wartime Leader of Bosnian Serbs Receives 27-Year Sentence," *New York Times*, 28 Sept. 2006.
2. *Ibid.*

CHAPTER 11

1. Lydia Polgreen, "A Country and a Continent, Hanging in the Balance," *New York Times*, 23 Jan. 2006: A4.
2. Panel discussion, "Mimesis Creativity and Reconciliation," *Colloquium on Violence & Religion Conference*. Ottawa, Canada. 31 May – 4 Jun. 2006.

CHAPTER 12

1. President George W. Bush. [State of the Union Address] United States. The White House. Office of the Press Secretary (January 29, 2002).
2. CNN, "Saddam addresses Iraqi people." Baghdad, Iraq. 20 Mar. 2003 www.cnn.com/2003/WORLD.
3. Girard, *Job* 9.

CHAPTER 13

1. Arun Ghandi. Letter to Richard Sanders, Coordinator of the Coalition to Oppose the Arms Trade. www.gandhiinstitute.org.
2. Bob Herbert, "An Invisible War," *New York Times*, 3 May 2007.
3. Manohla Dargis, "Ghastly Conflagration, Tormented Aftermath," *New York Times*, 20 Oct. 2006: B21.
4. Sabrina Tavernise, "Cycle of Revenge Fuels a Pattern of Iraqi Killings," *New York Times*, 20 Nov. 2006.
5. www.gandhiinstitute.org.
6. www.gandhiinstitute.org.
7. www.gandhiinstitute.org.

CHAPTER 14

1. Jennifer Saranow, "A Few Centuries Late, Convicted Witches Gain New Defenders," *Wall Street Journal*, 15 Sept. 2006: 1.
2. Laurie Goodstein, "Disowning Conservative Politics, Evangelical Pastor Rattles Flock," *New York Times*, 30 Jul. 2006: 1.
3. *Ibid.*
4. Francis Sejersted, Chairman of the Norwegian Nobel Committee, "Presentation Speech, Nobel Peace Prize 1991," The Nobel Foundation, 1991. http://nobelprize.org/nobel_prizes/peace/laureates/1991/presentation-speech.html.
5. African National Congress, "Profile of Nelson Rolihlahla Mandela," 21 May, 2007. www.anc.org.za/people/mandela.html.

6. Daniel Gilbert, "He Who Cast the First Stone Probably Didn't," *New York Times*, 24 Jul. 2006: 19.
7. *Ibid.*
8. Stephanie Preston and Frans B. M. de Wall, "Empathy: Its Ultimate and Proximate Bases," *Behavioral and Brain Sciences*, 25 Feb. 2002:1-20. This article summarizes a study by J. H. Masserman, S. Wechkin, W. Terris, "'Altruistic' Behavior in Rhesus Monkeys," *American Journal of Psychiatry* 121 (1964): 584-85.
9. James K.A. Smith, "Sightings: Our History of Violence," *Circa: News From the University of Chicago Divinity School*, Spring 2006, Number 25: 9.
10. *Ibid.*
11. James Alison, "The Anatomy of Reconciliation," Conference at Trinity Church 1 Wall Street, Trinity Institute. 2006.

APPENDIX

APPENDIX I
A TRAVELER'S GUIDE

CREED OF COMPASSION

- I am limited.
- True peace is universal peace.
- Violence or the abuse of another human being can never be justified.

CREED OF SELF-WORSHIP

- I believe in one god – myself.
- The fulfillment of my desires is the ultimate good.
- Anyone or anything that gets in the way of the fulfillment of my desires is my enemy and is subject to destruction by any means available.

MYTHOLOGICAL RULE #1

Evil can and must be identified with absolute certainty.

Assumptions Behind Rule #1:

- Evil is somewhere outside our community.
- We have the right and responsibility to destroy it.
- Only then will we have peace.

MYTHOLOGICAL RULE #2

We know we are good because we hate evil.

MYTHOLOGICAL RULE #3
There are two kinds of violence – Good Violence and Bad Violence.

MYTHOLOGICAL RULE #4
Sacrificial Formula: Someone can be sacrificed for my good or the good of my community. The End justifies the Means.

Wicked TRUTH #1
Everyone is capable of being both good and evil.

Wicked TRUTH #2
Evil hides by accusing innocent others of being evil.

Wicked TRUTH #3
There is no Good Violence or Bad Violence; there is only violence.

Wicked TRUTH #4
The means become the end.

APPENDIX II
GLOSSARY

Myth: According to René Girard, Myths are the stories that get told by winners to deliberately conceal the losers' story. Myths both tell and conceal truth. They tell the truth that the winners feel a sense of security and safety at the defeat of their enemy. But Myths also conceal a truth – that the defeated enemy was an innocent victim, unfairly accused and violently silenced.

Popularity: A position on the top of the social pyramid. It is the result of being held in unanimous high esteem. Unpopularity is being held in unanimous low esteem.

Prophet: Often prophets are thought of as visionaries with a special power to foretell the future. While there is an element of fortune-telling involved, prophetic insights come not from some mystical power, but from a keen ability to see those things that are hidden from others. Prophets see clearly what we are blind to, not only the truths of our present behavior, but also the future consequences of the path we are on.

Sacrificial: Describes the willingness of a person or system to sacrifice some one or some group to achieve their aims.

Sacrificial Formula: The name given to the mechanism of Mythological Rule #4—The End justifies the Means. It allows for the suffering or death of one person for the benefit of the many. If the aim is believed to be good, then any means, even those of oppression and violence, can be justified. Same as *Scapegoat Mechanism*.
Sacrificial System: A code of conduct that depends on the Sacrificial Formula and asserts that the end justifies the means.

Scapegoat: A scapegoat is a person or group who is used by the community to cleanse itself of its internal conflicts. Whether or not the scapegoat is actually innocent or guilty of any evil is irrelevant (see Structural Innocence). Everyone within the community, however, must agree that the charge of evil is true.

Scapegoat Mechanism: See *Sacrificial Formula.*

Structural Innocence: This refers to the function of a scapegoat. A scapegoat is used to cleanse a community of its anger and resentments, though he is not the cause of that anger and resentment. He might be technically guilty of a crime, but he is structurally innocent of the accusation of evil made against him by a community that is using him to achieve peace.

Text of Persecution: Unlike a Myth, a Text of Persecution is an account of a scapegoating event that does not completely conceal the truth what happened. It has the potential to reveal that the "evil one" was actually an innocent victim of violence.

Unconditional Giving: Giving that asks for nothing in return. Same as unconditional love.

Violence: Myth claims that there are two types of violence. Good Violence is when good people kill bad people. Bad Violence is when bad people kill good people. The *Wicked* Truth reveals that such a distinction is a false one. From outside the Myth, violence is always bad and can never be a cause of celebration.

Wickedness: The little ways every day we fail to love one another and slip instead into hurtful patterns of gossip, blaming, resentments, and fits of anger.

APPENDIX III
RENÉ GIRARD

The following is a biography of the contemporary scholar, René Girard, taken from the website devoted to the study and advancement of his theory about violence, religion, and the origins of human culture.

RENÉ GIRARD
Honorary Chair of COV&R

René Girard was born in the southern French city of Avignon on Christmas day in 1923. Between 1943 and 1947, he studied in Paris at the École des Chartres, an institution for the training of archivists and historians, where he specialized in medieval history. In 1947 he went to Indiana University on a year's fellowship and eventually made almost his entire career in the United States. He completed a PhD in history at Indiana University in 1950 but also began to teach literature, the field in which he would first make his reputation. He taught at Duke University and at Bryn Mawr before becoming a professor at Johns Hopkins in Baltimore. In 1971 he went to the State University of New York at Buffalo for five years, returned to Johns Hopkins, and then finished his academic career at Stanford University where he taught between 1981 and his retirement in 1995.

Girard continues to lecture and write and still offers a seminar at Stanford, where he and his wife Martha make their home. In 1990, friends and colleagues of Girard's established the Colloquium on Violence and Religion to further research and discussion about the themes of Girard's work. The Colloquium meets annually either in Europe or the United States.

AWARDS & HOUNORS

Guggenheim Fellow (1960, 1967)
Modern Language Association Award (1965)
Honorary doctor of the Frije Universiteit Amsterdam (1985)
Honorary doctor of the University of Innsbruck/Austria (1988)
Honorary doctor of the Université d'Anvers/Belgium (1995)
Grand prix de philosophie de l'Académie française pour l'ensemble de son œuvre (1996)
Nonino Literary Prize, Italy (1998)
Honorary doctor of the University of Padova/Italy (2001)
Member of the Académie française (March 2005)

IF YOU ARE INTERESTED IN FURTHER READING, HERE IS A PARTIAL LIST OF BOOKS BY RENÉ GIRARD:

The Scapegoat (1982), trans. Yvonne Freccero. (Baltimore, MD: Johns Hopkins University Press, 1986).

Things Hidden Since the Foundation of the World (1978), with Jean-Michel Oughourlian and Guy Lefort, trans. Stephen Bann and Michael Metteer. (Stanford, CA: Stanford University Press, 1987).

Violence and the Sacred (1972), trans. Patrick Gregory. (Baltimore, MD: Johns Hopkins University Press, 1977).

THE FOLLOWING BOOKS ARE WRITTEN BY OTHER AUTHORS ABOUT GIRARD'S THEORY AND ARE VERY HELPFUL AS AN INTRODUCTION TO HIS IDEAS:

Bailie, Gil *Violence Unveiled.* (New York, NY: The Crossroad Publishing Company, 1997).

Fleming, Chris *René Girard: Violence and Mimesis*. (Cambridge: Polity Press, 2004).

If you'd like to find other books and authors or to learn more about the scholarly research being done across academic disciplines, you can go to the Colloquium on Violence and Religion (COV&R) website: theol.uibk.ac.at/cover.

ABOUT THE AUTHOR

Suzanne Ross has worked in education for over fifteen years, first teaching Montessori preschool and kindergarten and then working as a corporate training consultant. Currently, Suzanne works as the education director for a United Church of Christ congregation. In 1997, she came across the work of René Girard and was astounded at how his theory illuminated so much of her life and work as an educator, a parent, a church member, and a lover of fiction and theater. She is a member of the Colloquium on Violence & Religion, the academic group dedicated to exploring the applications of Girard's work, and she has attended and presented at the annual conferences. In January 2007, she and her husband Keith founded The Raven Foundation to increase awareness of Girardian theory and *The Wicked Truth* is an example of the Foundation's work. Suzanne and Keith live in Glenview, Illinois, near their two married children and work together at The Raven Foundation. You can visit the Foundation at www.ravenfoundation.org.